"THE BUTTERFLY"

"…old things are passed away; behold, all things are become new."
– 2 Corinthians 5:17

Butterflies are common in Christian iconography. Early Christianity absorbed some ancient icons into itself and possibly borrowed cocoon/butterfly symbology from ancient Egypt as ancient Egyptians realized funeral wrappings of mummies resembled cocoons, and butterflies represented souls flying free into the Afterlife. Christian tradition views the butterfly as a symbol of new life. A caterpillar's metamorphosis is a wonderful illustration of transformation and resurrection. In some spiritual circles, the butterfly represents the spirit or soul. Symbolically, butterflies are creatures with the ability to transcend the ordinary and take flight above the commonplace.

For Verna's transformation into her new life – her "transcendence from the ordinary" – in this final book in the OVERCOMING series, the ancient symbol of a butterfly is quite apt. Already "above the commonplace" as an LPN who became an expressly-requested OR scrub nurse by renowned surgeons and then a Teamster on a newspaper's loading dock, Verna "spreads her wings" and soars into her soul-satisfying skies as an accomplished guitarist, songwriter, and performer. From an abusive marriage, a journey through encumbering Welfare, the conundrum of adoption or abortion due to a pregnancy by rape, rigors of Nursing School, progressing to high skills of an Operating Room Nurse, descending into catatonia to be revived through music, experiencing a second disastrous marriage, and becoming the first woman to work on a Seattle newspaper's loading dock, Verna blossoms into the extraordinary talent whose seed was planted in her young childhood spirit's fertile soil. Though this series ends, her story continues. It is a remarkable one!

"Just like the butterfly, I, too, will awaken in my own time."

– thevintageangel.com

"The Lord is my strength and my shield; my heart trusted in him, and I am helped: therefore my heart greatly rejoiceth; and with my song will I praise him." – Psalm 28:7

The Story of Verna Louise Williams

OVERCOMING

"My Heart Greatly Rejoiceth"

Book Five

The Story of Verna Louise Williams

OVERCOMING

"My Heart Greatly Rejoiceth"

An Autobiographical Fiction

VASHTI ATAYA

Book Five

XULON PRESS

Xulon Press
2301 Lucien Way #415
Maitland, FL 32751
407.339.4217
www.xulonpress.com

THE STORY OF VERNA LOUISE WILLIAMS, OVERCOMING, "My Heart Greatly Rejoiceth," Book Five

Unless otherwise indicated, Scripture quotations taken from the King James Version (KJV) –*public domain.*

Printed in the United States of America.

ISBN-13: 978-1-6312-9173-9

DEDICATION

To my beautiful daughters. They are my butterflies.

"Butterflies are God's confetti, thrown upon the Earth in celebration of His love." – K. D'Angelo

ACKNOWLEDGEMENTS

There are so many people I would like to acknowledge, too many to put on one page. Of course, I always wish to acknowledge my Editor whose tireless, long hours at his computer shapes, molds, and forms these words as he whittles away deadwood to reveal my books' hearts and souls. I acknowledge and thank my Publisher, Xulon Press, for their unflagging support in my authorship and producing beautiful books within whose covers Verna's story rests, waiting for those covers to open so it can come alive once more. Certainly I always thank and acknowledge you, Dear Reader, for without you these words would be floating aimlessly in the Cosmos, dead words not read. It is you who ground them, move them, give them life. Through you, they live again.

This is the final book of the OVERCOMING series. It is the one in which Verna meets the miracle prepared for her from countless time. This book contains the beginnings of Verna's – of *my* – new life. Therefore, it is quite fitting that a special acknowledgement goes to a special person present at those beginnings, one whose extraordinary artistic talent is enjoyed by many, one whose loving support and encouragement significantly helped me launch into uncharted waters, one who was a dear friend and remains close in my heart – Clarice Keegan.

This series is "Autobiographical Fiction," meaning some characters may be fictional blends of actual people such as Geniece Krafts was in *"Joy Cometh In The Morning,"* Book One. In this book, however, Clarice was real. So was her daughter, Shanti. The late Tom Tichenor, Master Puppeteer, was also real. Though I never met him, Tom's contribution to my life through my husband was immeasurable. Thank you, Tom, for inspiring him and, in turn, inspiring me!

Sadly, Clarice is no longer among us, the living. Yet part of her soul remains in three of her paintings that hang on my walls. She is in the photographic portrait she took of me, the one that rests on an antique table in my living room. Much of her remains in my memory, never to be forgotten. I recall her sitting at my dining room table, joyfully showing her latest art works. Clarice was thrilled – jubilant – to know of my successful beginnings with my life-partner and dear husband, Noah, when we began our entertainment career as "The StorySingers." We could not have launched as successfully as we did had it not been for Clarice shooting promotional photographs of us. I know her spirit is just as jubilant and supportive of my authorship.

Perhaps a quote from the late British author, Sir Terence "Terry" Pratchett, says it well: "No one is actually dead until the ripples they cause in the world die away." Clarice's ripples never will.

Thank you, Clarice. Thank you for everything.

I must also acknowledge and thank Shanti who remains a dear friend. Shanti's support, then and now, is invaluable to me!

"To know God, watch a butterfly return to the same tree after a year and a thousand miles." – Jonathan Lockwood Huic

"We are all butterflies. Earth is our chrysalis." – LeeAnn Taylor

"If nothing ever changed, there would be no such things as butterflies." – Wendy Mass

"Go on, hitch a ride on the back of a butterfly. There's no better way to fly." – Patrick Monahan

"O clap your hands, all ye people; shout unto God with a voice of triumph." – Psalm 47:1

AUTOBIOGRAPHICAL FICTION

The OVERCOMING Series is presented as Autobiographical Fiction.

Webster's Dictionary defines Autobiographical as "the biography of a person narrated by himself or herself." Webster's defines Fiction as "something invented by the imagination or feigned."

The storyline of the OVERCOMING Series is based upon actual, true, and real events in the author's life. This is the "Autobiographical" component.

Various names are altered; some characters are combinations of real persons, and some conversations are "something invented by the imagination." This is the "Fictional" component.

Blending both elements in Autobiographical Fiction, the OVERCOMING Series tells the author's true story through her fictional avatar, Verna Louise Williams.

"THE STORY OF VERNA LOUISE WILLIAMS, OVERCOMING" SERIES

"Joy Cometh In The Morning," Book One
"A beautiful and inspirational story." – Vikki McRaven, Author
"...a full and vibrant story." – Salem Author Services

"The Trees Shall Clap Their Hands," Book Two
"...an enjoyable and captivating reading experience..." – Salem Author Servies

"Then Do We With Patience Wait," Book Three
"...a compelling narrative with rich characters and settings..." – Salem Author Services

"The Valley Of The Shadow," Book Four
"...a balanced, flowing pace...both informative and eloquently written..." – Salem Author Services

TABLE OF CONTENTS

INTRODUCTION

"The Lord is my strength and my shield; my heart trusted in him,
and I am helped: therefore my heart greatly rejoiceth; and with
my song will I praise him." – Psalm 28:7

This is the fifth and final book of the OVERCOMING series, "The Story of Verna Louise Williams." Throughout her story, Verna's heart indeed trusted in her God, her strength and shield, and she was helped many times over by her steadfast faith. As she progressed from an abusive marriage, through Welfare's morass, miseries of a high-risk inexplicable pregnancy, constraints of nursing school, catastrophic loss of her daughters through deception, victories as a respected OR Nurse, and a second miserable marriage to bloom as a talented musician and entertainer who touched the hearts and lives of literally thousands, Verna always kept a song in her heart. Her heart's song ever praised her God and continues to do so.

For Verna's story is *my* story, and it has been humbling to write it. It has also been a renewing – a renewing of faith in the absolutely amazing "Mysterious Ways of God, His Wonders to perform!" Although partly fictional in some names, places, conversations, and events, this series' basic storyline is factual. For example, "Oak Creek United Methodist Church" in the series is a fictional name, but Verna's – *my* – participation in the actual church was real. "Mesquite Valley Mental Hospital" in Book 4 is a fictional name, but Verna's – *my* – experiences in the actual facility were real. Nursing school and OR involvement were real. Verna meeting Norman as she did – *my meeting my sweet Noah* – was real. Verna's dream of the stuffed sleeping bag – *my dream* – was real. The list goes on. And on. And on. Verna's story is truly one of a life's journey laced with miracles.

It is difficult to assign a "level of miracle-ness" to a miracle, for each and every one is a wonder in itself. If possible to assign such a status, however, the "miracle of the catalytic converter" within this book would perhaps be unsurpassed. It was huge! And it was *real!*

Verna's story is also one birth mother's story – a true story of adoption as an instrument of both profound joy and overwhelming sorrow. Her story is one of overcoming incredible challenges, both societal and personal. Hers is a story of deep determination, dogged grit, and resolute single-mindedness to push through all obstructions and to surmount all barriers – to overcome. Undergirding it all,

Verna's story – *my story* – is one of inspiration. Dating back centuries, "to inspire" had a theological meaning of literally drawing in the breath of God. "Inspiration" still has the connotation of a mystical power beyond the human self to move a mind into a creative, receptive state. This series has inspired me once again to remember the miracles through which I lived.

In the 1981 movie "Excalibur" after Arthur's final victory, Merlin appears in the midst of the rejoicing knights, quiets them, and says, "Remember it well, then…this night. For it is the doom of men that they forget." It is my hope that this series has helped you, Dear Reader, to remember *your* miracles as I have remembered mine. For it *is* our doom to forget them.

Let's remember. Let's allow our hearts to greatly rejoice. And let's let our songs forever praise!

"Sometimes good things fall apart so better things can fall together." –
Marilyn Monroe

RHODODENDRONS

Chilly droplets from a steely sky hung in the air, not quite rain, but not quite fog, either – more like a vapory condensation, a dewy haze, a frosty steam. Driving through that cold, wintry mist of a somber Pacific Northwest gloomy-gray December day might have been depressing were it not for the rainbow dropping from a hole in the leaden overcast – a rarely-seen natural phenomenon of winter's sullen skies perhaps, but also a possible portent of good fortune awaiting her in Seattle. She hoped it signified such; there are supposed to be pots of gold at ends of rainbows, so they say. Maybe she could find hers in the fabled city; perchance it rested at the foot of the Space Needle. She had left Tucson once again in search of a new life, this time with a new husband and no daughters, this time headed northwest instead of southeast.

Six years ago in 1970 – *Oh, my God,* she thought, *all of this has happened in only six years?* – Verna escaped a horrific abusive marriage in Tucson. After her divorce, with her two small daughters, she fled for the safety of Orlando, thanks to the generosity of her dear Tucson friend, Janice Sawtelle, who provided airfare. It was in Orlando her father, Frank Davidson, and her mother, Arlene, Oklahoma transplants now Florida "natives," helped her rent an apartment. It was there she qualified for Florida Welfare and "made ends meet" by taking in ironing, an arduous, laborious task which emptied her of energy. It was in Orlando she was raped, experienced a draining, high-risk pregnancy, birthed a baby girl who, miraculously and telepathically, identified herself as "Chrissy," and whom Verna gave up for adoption. The aching emptiness of losing Chrissy never left her, nor did her anguish over her ex-husband Patrick's devious deception that allowed his current wife, Anne Marie, to legally adopt her daughters, Susanna and Veronica – to literally, sneakily *snatch them away from her!* Now her daughters lived once again with *him*…and *her*…in Tucson.

While in Orlando, Verna, after herculean laboring through nursing school to triumphantly graduate number five in her class of sixty-eight, rose to become an esteemed, surgeon-requested Operating Room Scrub Nurse in Orlando's prestigious Orange Memorial Hospital. She diligently saved her money to return to Tucson and fight for the legal return of her daughters taken from her by her bitter ex-husband's deceitful duplicity. Although eager to return to Arizona, Verna learned to wait with patience for the right time…God's Time, not hers…to leave Florida. Indeed she took comfort in Solomon's wisdom in Ecclesiastes. "To everything there is a season, and a time to every purpose under the heaven." Times such as a hysterectomy due to uterine fibroids, her father's passing, and circumstances of vacating her apartment so a friend in need could rent it, kept her from departing.

In those "times to every purpose under the heaven" she grasped once again God's work in His Mysterious Ways to perform His Wonders. A year ago on December first, this very month, her passenger jetliner lifted off from Orlando International as it carried her, once again, to Tucson. She could never have imagined the Wondrous Miracle God was preparing for her through His Mysterious Ways.

For when she was once more in Arizona, Verna encountered her deepest distress as she descended into catatonia. It was in this "time and purpose" her musical spirit began to stir as "Amazing Grace" reached down into her darkness, flicked on a light, and led her shattered self to wholeness. Music Therapist Tom Nation played "Amazing Grace" on his guitar and softly sang it one night after the music therapy session ended; Verna, sitting unresponsive and stone still, started singing also as the old hymn touched true, deep depths within and awakened her once more. It was within the walls of Mesquite Valley Mental Hospital she met her psychological salvation as well as fellow patient, Gerald Hansen, who would become her second husband.

After their respective releases from Mesquite Valley, Jerry and Verna married in Las Vegas. He applied for and was accepted as an electronics engineer for the National Oceanic and Atmospheric Administration, headquartered in Seattle. For the second time, Verna left Arizona in search of a new life, seeking it in Seattle as she once sought it in Orlando. Now she sat in the passenger seat of their relatively new tan Dodge van as they drove into the cold mist-veiled city, a lone rare winter's rainbow dripping before them, both of them singing softly, "Look, look, look to the rainbow. Follow it over the hill and the stream. Look, look, look to the rainbow. Follow the fellow who follows a dream." Jerry was following his dream of being a NOAA engineer; Verna's dream was to return to work as an Operating Room Nurse, a position which significantly fulfilled her. She had no way of knowing she was driving into a dream which would fill her soul's cup to overflowing.

Dearest Moma,

Well, here we are in Seattle. It's so big! We're in the rental house that we arranged for over the phone before we left Arizona. There are several things that are very disappointing. Jerry chose it because it featured an attached double car garage, thinking he could store larger portions of our household goods there, the stuff still in boxes; that way we wouldn't have to completely unpack until we select a house and buy it. Well, the garage door is buckled and does not work, so we can't get anything big in there. The garage floor is dirt! Can you imagine! And, it's damp in there as, apparently, it rains all the time in Seattle and the roof leaks. So our boxes and things are crammed into this small, furnished rental house. Jerry did uncrate the piano, though, so it looms in the middle of the tiny living room. Jerry plays it to calm himself. Lately, he plays it a lot.

Neither of us is accustomed to constantly being cold. I was given a pair of red fleece long-johns with a trapdoor in the back as a gag gift, and I've barely taken them off since we left Tucson. The trip here over the Grapevine in California was kinda, well, hairy in places. The road kept icing up and all I can think of is that our guardian angels worked overtime to keep the van from sliding off the mountain highways.

This is a two story house with an attic bedroom featuring two built-in captain's beds upstairs. All the warm air rises so we sleep up there under the sloping roof. I sleep in my long-johns and zipped up in my down sleeping bag. There is a fireplace in the living room, and I've already burned through nearly all the wood that we found stacked in the damp garage in an effort to take the chill off this house. Serves us right for renting sight unseen, I guess.

Jerry is settling in well at NOAA, and very excited about his upcoming first time out at sea on board one of the NOAA ships. Our plan is to buy a house before he goes so that I will be settled here someplace more comfortable than this.

There is a nursing home within walking distance so I plan to go there and put in an application. We just have the one vehicle, the faithful tan Dodge van that carried us here. I love driving it. Jerry has found a spot in a carpool so I have the use of it during the day. Once I get somewhat settled, I plan to place applications for OR Nurse at the hospitals downtown.

Seattle is really amazing. It reminds me a little bit of Germany where we lived when I was so little. Tall evergreen trees everywhere, a chilly light mist settles on your face when you're outside, and it has snow covered mountains all around it. Not as spectacular as the real Alps maybe, but spectacular enough. It's overcast most of the time, and when the sun shines and the sky's blue, you can see the mountains. That's called "when the mountains are out." But the overcast is supposed to be good for photography. The overcast is called "oyster light" because the sky looks like the silver-gray inside of an oyster shell. They call the almost constant drizzle "Scotch mist" because Scotland is also damp and misty. But it's beautiful here.

I hope you and Robert are well. I'm glad you married again after Daddy passed. Besides being in the Masonic Lodge with Daddy, Robert was always a very good friend to you both. Him being a widower, and you being a widow, I think your marriage is a good thing. Are you getting used to being called "Mrs. Carrolton?"

One of the things I plan to do before Jerry sets sail is to get a good dog. I've always felt that a good dog at hand is the best thing for a woman alone. So I'm watching the papers for ads and feel confident that God will guide me to the one that is for me.

Love,
Your Daughter, Verna Louise

The realtor, Mr. Jenkins, stood in the gravel driveway of the fifth house they'd seen that day. "Well, whaddaya think? It's within your price range…meets all the details you gave me…at the end of a dead end street…has trees. And you said you didn't want anything real big, so a two bedroom, one bath home seems just right." He looked back and forth at Jerry and Verna, eager to make the sale and be done with them. Verna was still exhausted from the long drive over the mountains, being constantly cold in the rental house, and Jerry's fear of the unknown. He wanted to buy a house but was reluctant to spend money. They had seen dozens. *Dozens!* But Jerry always found *something* wrong with each one. The man standing before them in the tan raincoat was the latest in a long line of realtors who had shown them houses. At this point, Verna would have happily settled for a cardboard box. She looked at Jerry. With hope. With encouragement. With resolve.

Eyes on the ground, every third breath a "humphing sigh," lost in indecision, he twisted and tangled his long fingers like a den of slithering snakes, coiling over and around each other. At times Verna glimpsed the mental patient she first met in Mesquite Valley Mental Hospital; this was one of those times.

Verna smiled at their realtor. "Mr. Jenkins, could we have a word alone? Please give us a minute, won't you?" He nodded obligingly and went to his car.

"Jerry, I don't see anything wrong with this house. We didn't know real estate here was so much more expensive than in Arizona. But we have enough for a down payment, and then maybe in a year or two, we'll know the area better, choose a different location, and who knows? Maybe we'll build one exactly like we want." Verna looked at him hopefully. "There's a nice Methodist church close by. We can finally settle into our own church home together. And I saw a lovely park just over the way. You did tell me you plan to start running every morning, didn't you?" Verna hugged him. They shivered in the January chill, Jerry's almost six-foot frame nearly enveloped Verna's five-foot-five-inch one, impeded by his round bump of a belly. Verna couldn't tell if his brown eyes watered from cold or fear…or *both*! He released her, looked at the ground, and hesitantly spoke as a child might speak to a parent.

"Wellll...yeah...I reckon…yeah,..I reckon we *do* have 'nough fer tha down payment...I guess...prob'ly…" Then quickly, as if excusing his reticence, "But this don't seem like much of a house fer what we coulda got in Tucson. I mean, look…" Jerry scanned the area. "See. It's got all these big green bushes growing ever'where, an', look, they prac'lly cover all them windows!" He gestured at the front of the house. "An' it don't have a fireplace, an' how do we know them electric baseboard heaters'll even keep tha place warm? I mean…Y'know?...How do we know?" He shrugged himself deeper into his parka, sighed again, looked down, and scuffed his size 11 feet on the driveway gravel.

Verna appraised the yard, taking in the very tall pine tree smack in the middle, the hugely-overgrown green bushes along the front wall and around the corner, and what appeared to be some kind of fruit tree by the front door. "Well, maybe we can get some pruning shears and tame these bushes. And, know what? We can always get you a pair of red fleece long-johns like mine if we can't keep the house warm enough for you," she laughed. "Come on, Jerry. It's a perfectly fine house. It's easy to get to I-5 from here, and, once you get on I-5 you can get just about anywhere in Seattle. You'll have your carpool, and I'll drive the van. Or, if I work downtown, catch the bus at the park'n'ride we saw. We'll be okay. You'll see." Verna smiled at her new husband.

Jerry looked at her, gazing thoughtfully, trying to remember the mute, stone-still, catatonic, pallid mental patient who had become this vivacious, shimmering brown-haired, sparkling green-eyed, lovely woman. "You think so?" He glanced around the yard again. "You think we can be happy here? I mean, It's not very big...an'...them baseboard heaters don't look like much...an'...an'..." His words trailed off in a surrendered sigh, and his shoulders slumped in weary acquiescence. "Well...yeah...okay. If you think this'll do, let's...let's do it!"

"Well, that's tha las' load. Good thing we had tha van, huh? Saved us having ta hire movers ta get all our other stuff over here from tha rental house, didn't it?" Jerry grinned. The only thing crated and moved was the piano, and it was already in the family room.

Verna grimaced. She had tugged and pulled on boxes all day, and her back hurt. "Yeah. Sure saved us some money, all right." She sighed and looked around. The little house at the end of the dead end street was small, yes, but their down payment had reduced the monthly mortgage payments considerably, so they could live here and still meet Jerry's sizable child support requirements. "Let's see about an estimate on putting in a chain link fence. Once we get a fence up, I can get a dog, as we discussed."

Jerry's head snapped around. "A dog? You *really* plan ta get a dog? I mean... think-a tha costs...it'll need vet care...it'll need ta go ta tha groomer...it'll need dog food...water dish...collar...leash...you know. *Costs!*" Jerry looked nervous. And more than a little irritable.

By now Verna had learned to mollify him much as she once pacified surgeons in operating rooms. "Pay is higher here than in Tucson, and I will make more money than I used to. We'll be more than able to afford the expense. Besides, think how lonesome it will be for me here without you. You'll be onboard a ship filled with scientists, specialists, other technical people like yourself. I'll be..." Verna gestured at the yard "...here." She sighed. "Alone. A woman alone needs a good dog. My grandmother was widowed three times and reared her five living children alone on a big farm with only a farm dog for help. Now, I don't have five children, and this is not a farm. But I am kinda down here alone at the end of a dead end street. I need a good dog." She smiled at him. The pros and cons flitted across his face as she watched. Finally, she saw a faint flush of agreement.

"A dog. Yeah. Good idea. He can bark an' warn you in case there's any...any... people or animals that might be...around." He looked at his shoes. "An' he can keep ya company...I guess."

"Excellent. I'll look into breeders. I want a really good dog. Since I grew up with a German Shepherd, I'll look at shepherd kennels." Verna went into the house, shedding her parka as she went.

Once again, as she had when she left Orlando for Tucson, Verna encountered hospitals not hiring LPNs for the OR. She was determined to work in her desired field or not at all. One dark, rainy, late February afternoon, after a series of job interviews wherein she was offered nursing positions other than the OR, she drove past a red neon sign that read "Aurora Veterinary Clinic." The sign featured a dog barking at a cat climbing a pole, rippling neon lights energizing the cat.

Hmmm...a veterinary hospital...with a neon sign...wonder if the vet would consider an LPN/Operating Room Nurse...as an assistant...

Verna circled the block and turned in, adept at maneuvering and parking the one ton van. She was now accustomed to the fine, damp "Scotch mist," the constant chill, (she practically lived in her parka and long johns) and driving on wet pavement with the ever-present swish-swish of windshield wipers. She went inside the waiting area and, seeing no one behind the counter, sat in one of the cushioned vinyl chairs and leaned back. It smelled reassuringly like a vet hospital; animal odors, combined with the smells of disinfectants, medicine, and pet food swirled in the warm air. Verna loved and appreciated warm air, no matter how it smelled. She missed the fireplace in the rental house.

A man appeared from a door behind the counter. Medium tall, young looking, handsome, brown hair, friendly brown eyes, wearing a zippered white smock over a crisp white shirt, and striped navy blue and white tie, he smiled in her direction.

"Hi, there. How can I help you?"

Verna stood and removed her parka. "Hello. I'm Verna Louise Hansen. Do you need a vet assistant?"

Startled, the man froze. His smile stayed in place, but there was confusion behind it. "What? How...how did you know I needed an assistant? I haven't advertised." He looked at her, puzzled.

"Well, I was just returning home from some job interviews in downtown Seattle, and I saw your sign. I worked all through high school for our local veterinarian in Oklahoma, Doctor Kelsey, and also for Doctor Davis, a veterinarian in Orlando the year I was in Nursing School. I really miss the work, and just thought I'd ask." Verna smiled. "So, do you need an assistant?"

"Actually, I do. Or rather, I will. Today, my current assistant, Rachel, learned she is expecting, and plans to leave the position. She just gave me two weeks' notice before she left for the day." He grinned at Verna and glanced at his watch. "Just now. Nursing School, did you say? Are you a nurse?" "Yes." He beckoned to her and opened the gate in the counter. "Come on back and let's talk."

Doctor Griffin, wearing an almost silly expression, barely believing his good fortune, sat in a leather chair in his cluttered office across from Verna. She described her LPN experience, her special OR training, her OR work in Orlando's Orange Memorial, and in Tucson's Saint Joseph's. She told him of her applications in the local hospitals and how none would accept an LPN for that position. Now she sat quietly, waiting.

"Well, I suppose I ought to talk to my associate, Doctor Kurtzmann, but his day off is today, and he isn't here." He shrugged and waved his hands in the air indicating his absence. Doctor Griffin drummed his fingers on the desk a moment. "What kind of salary are you seeking?"

Verna explained her salary as an OR Nurse at Orange Memorial in Orlando and Saint Joe's in Tucson. He grinned. "I can do that." He stood. Can you start a week from Monday?"

"Sure. But how 'bout I come on in tomorrow and start learning the ropes from...uh...Rachel? Is that her name?" She shook hands with him. "No charge. I love the animals, so I'll be happy to be here.

"How do you do, Frau Frisch? I am Verna Louise Hansen. We spoke on the phone?" Verna looked around at the clean, orderly kennel grounds as she met the owner of Volker Kennels. Doctor Griffin had recommended her. She brought all of her puppies to his clinic.

"Ya, ya, hello, hello. I am pleased to meet you." She pumped Verna's hand, European style, up, down, up, release. "Dis vay...right ofer heah..." She led Verna into the interior of her large house and through a second door. "Dis is mein velping room. Ven I haf' a bitch ready to velp, I bring her in heah so she vill be varm und cosy. Isn't dat right, Schatzi-Lein, ya?" She lovingly petted the head of a large German Shepherd female lying in a bed of clean shredded newspapers in a big cedar box. A nervous young man attended her and didn't seem to want Verna to approach too close. Respectfully, she kept her distance.

"Look! Look look look! Heah come za virst puppy! See? Ya?" The mother dog immediately began licking the puppy as it squirmed with newborn squeals. It rooted, soon latched on to a nipple, and began suckling. Frau Frisch produced two folding chairs and invited Verna to join her. They sat companionably together during the birth of eight puppies. "She is vun uff mein best mutters," crooned the kennel owner. "I used to show her, but she prefers to be heah at home razzer den New York," the woman smiled modestly. "She is a champion. As is der puppies' sire, Volker. Ya." She gestured to a photograph of a handsome German Shepherd in front of a trophy table, blue ribbon on his collar. "He von best in breed, und von all der obedience trials. He vorks as a search und rescue dog, now, ven he isn't busy becoming a papa to dese fine pups. Ve named der business after him." She smiled, showing yellowed teeth. "Or, rather, mein husband did. He died last year." Her face saddened for a moment but she brightened at the birth of the next puppy.

Verna watched the behavior of the entire litter. She chose the firstborn. A female. Since her sire was a champion dog who went on quests to rescue people, Verna named her, "Questra." In the ensuing weeks, she made several trips to the kennel to visit the puppy before she was old enough to come home. Questra was fine, plump, strong, and healthy, and Verna loved her more than she'd loved anything in her life except her children.

Questra lay at her feet in the dining area while Verna drank her second cup of coffee. It was late March, but still chilly. The electric baseboard heaters worked fine to make the house nice and cozy. Jerry was at sea. Verna was busy with her new job at the Aurora vet clinic, as well as training her beautiful puppy. Housebreaking had been no problem, since Verna had no distractions and understood when Questra wanted to go out. Long ago her dad told her that housebreaking puppies was a matter of learning to interpret their signals and acting accordingly. "It's all about communication, see," said her dad. "Dogs're smart. Clean. They don't wanna foul their home any more'n you want 'em to, so you show 'em where outside is, and they'll tell you when they want to go there."

Verna laid her newspaper aside, and Questra immediately sat up. "Ah...you want to go play, don't you, Girl." The beautiful dog yipped a very puppy-sounding yip. "Well, so do I. Let's get the ball and let's go play." The nylon shell rustled as Verna slid her arms into the neon orange lining of the navy blue parka. Now Questra yapped, woofed, and danced excitedly. She knew the parka meant they were going outside, which meant fun. In the yard, as she ran and played in the morning mist and caught the ball, silvery drops of moisture collected in her dark fur, spangling it with crystals. Tail high, wagging vigorously, she brought the ball back and dropped it at Verna's feet, pink tongue lolling in a happy doggy grin. "Questra, sit." The dog lowered her hind quarters to the ground and looked at her human expectantly. Verna picked up the ball and tossed it to the far end of the yard near the new chain link fence. City ordinance dictated it could only be four feet high, but it defined Questra's territory.

After another few minutes of play, Verna took the ball in the house, emptied the last of the coffee pot into her travel mug, and grabbed her keys off the wall hook. Hearing the rattle of the keys, Questra pranced expectantly to the gate. She went to work with Verna every day, sitting in the passenger seat, gazing out the window.

Jerry may have a whole shipload of people, but I have Questra...I think I have it better than he does...

"Verna, I'm going to need your help. Spaying a Saint Bernard is a lot like performing a hysterectomy on a woman, so I'd appreciate your assistance," said Doctor Kurtzmann. Doctor Griffin's associate had really "taken to" Verna. Together they were a good team. "Sure thing, Doctor K. I have everything ready. I'll just go get our patient."

Verna lifted her easily from her kennel and took her to the scale. "One hundred eight pounds." She laid her gently on the stainless steel surgical table. The dog wagged her tail and looked at Verna expectantly, probably wondering where breakfast was. Verna talked to her as she always did to animals in her care. "Yes, you are a good girl, a wonderful girl, and you are so pretty!" Gently she held her left arm under her patient's chin and extended the dog's right front leg, thumb over the vein. Doctor Kurtzmann shaved a bit of hair from the crook, swabbed the skin with alcohol, and inserted the needle for the anesthetic. The tail wagging slowed and stopped. Verna stretched her out on her back, started the oxygen, and proceeded to shave the abdomen.

"Verna, how did it come about that a nurse like you chose to come work for us?" Doctor Kurtzmann snapped on his latex gloves and smiled over his surgical mask.

"Well, Doctor K, I guess I just prefer animals to people. Animals can't tell you where they hurt, but they sure can tell you they like you," grinned Verna over her own mask. She handed him the scalpel. Veterinary surgery wasn't exactly the same as human surgery, but it was very familiar to Verna. She felt somewhat odd to have come full circle like this, returning to the work she once did as a teenager in her Lawton, Oklahoma hometown; with a new skill set in place, she was very valuable to the animal hospital.

Incision made, she retracted the skin and handed the doctor instruments needed as he operated. A thump sounded overhead. Doctor K looked at the ceiling. "Ah. One of the tenants is awake."

Aurora Animal Hospital featured one-bedroom upstairs apartments for eight tenants, four of whom worked shifts at Boeing. "You can tell the time by which one's feet hit the floor first," chuckled Doctor Kurtzmann.

"How's that shepherd puppy of yours working out, Verna?" he asked as he fished out the uterus and tied it off. "Are you going to have her spayed?" He looked up as she handed him the suture.

"No. I think I'll have her bred at her second estrus, and then see about spaying her. Frau Frisch is very proud of her lineage, and I'm sure she'd like to have more like her."

Doctor Kurtzmann closed the skin incision with wire, and Verna pulled the IV needle and applied tape. The Saint Bernard nearly filled the surgical table. He was right. A spay procedure on a dog this size really was similar to doing a hysterectomy on a person.

"Well, have you told her yet about the ears?" He looked inquiringly at her.

"No, I haven't. Do you think it's genetic? I thought maybe it resulted from an injury from when she was in the litter." Verna put both arms under the dog to lift her off the table. The tongue was pinking, and the dog moved it a little. Their patient was starting to wake.

"I'll check her for you later, but I'm guessing it's genetic."

Questra's right ear didn't stand up as it should. It half flopped over, giving her a rather comical appearance that Verna found endearing. She didn't plan to show her dog, so she didn't mind that the ear didn't stand. But to a breeder it might be an indication of an undesirable trait.

Verna gently laid the sleeping Saint Bernard on a beach towel in the kennel and draped another towel over the front so it would shield her a bit from the noise and bright lights of the hospital.

Doctor Griffin called her from the reception area. A woman had arrived with three boisterous dogs for vaccinations and three equally ill-behaved children. Doctor Griffin looked a little overwhelmed. He and his wife had no children, so he always found them somewhat a nuisance.

"Let's work from Exam Two and keep them in Exam One so we can keep Reception clear," said the vet. With relief he went to the other exam room to wait while Verna brought the first dog.

And so it went. Aurora Clinic was a sizable practice, and Verna realized another person was also needed for the reception area. Although she hadn't been there long, she was treated with respect and appreciation; so she decided to voice such an opinion the next Monday meeting. The two vets were quite different in personality, but equally suited to veterinary medicine. Much had changed in the field since the sixties, but Verna was equal to every task asked of her. Her problem was there was only one of her.

In March the dark, claustrophobic bushes began budding, transforming the little house at the end of the road into a magical cottage surrounded by flowers in an enchanted glade. Smaller bushes at the base of the large plants flourished in shades of hot pink, orange, red, and white. The taller ones were festooned with blue, pink, white, and yellow blooms. Encircling the little house were rhododendrons bordered by azaleas in a riot of bright, colorful, beautiful, vibrant blossoms. It was a pale fairytale cottage in a gray dell, bordered by solemn dark-green trees, sitting amidst a kaleidoscope of brilliant color – a merge of grayscale and technicolor as if Dorothy in her pallid house had just opened the door to Oz. As Verna drove her solitary way home with the company of her dog in the passenger seat, she saw her secluded little dwelling with new eyes and breathed a prayer of thanksgiving.

Grandmother Davidson, you were right...there is always sunshine on your toast if you look for it...no sunshine here to speak of...but when I look at my house and those flowers...I see sunshine on my toast indeed...thank You, Heavenly Father, for guiding me here...

DOCTOR HALE

"**B**ut do you really think you need it? Psychiatric care, that is?" Jerry was packing for his next trip with NOAA. They would be in waters around Alaska, so he carefully folded and stacked warm clothes as he rolled turtlenecks into cylinders. Verna forced him to shop, finally convincing him such items were necessary. They both laughed when they found a pair of red fleece long-johns. "Don't laugh too hard. The day will come when you'll really, truly appreciate having them." She planted a firm kiss on his lips to seal in the laughter.

"I talked to Doctor Dodd in Tucson before we left, and he recommended I continue counseling. I'm completely off medications and holding together pretty good, don't you think?" She smiled at him as she handed him the new wool socks she'd made him buy. "But I went pretty far down the rabbit hole, as they say, and I don't ever want to go there again. Not if it can be helped by seeing a good doctor." They closed and latched the canvas suitcase. Verna put her arms around Jerry's neck. "I love you, you know. We found each other under pretty strange circumstances, so I think you understand better than anybody how important it is to maintain good mental health." She kissed him again. "So let's stay sane, how 'bout?"

"Well, yes, that's very logical. But how do you know this Doctor Hale's a good doctor?" Jerry shrugged, groping for words. "I mean...what if he somehow causes more harm than good?" They went into the kitchen for coffee. Now living in the chilly Pacific Northwest, they were quite enamored of good hot coffee. Verna enjoyed regular or decaf coffee with equal relish. She hadn't drunk iced coffee in a very long time. It was summer now, but she continued drinking her coffee hot.

"All I can do is make an appointment and go. I think I have enough experience with psychiatric types now to recognize a good doctor." She added cream to her cup and stirred. "I imagine after a few appointments I'll know whether to keep going or not." She looked at her husband. In her opinion, it was Jerry who really needed to be seeing a good doctor, but that was not possible under the circumstances. She knew he had odd little quirks – she'd seen them in the hospital. But, to her, it appeared they were becoming more pronounced. Paranoia about money was becoming alarming. Before setting sail, he signed checks to be sent to Salt Lake City, and Verna dated and mailed them as they became due. He reminded her multiple times about them and she finally had to say, "Look. I've got it. They'll go out on time. Enough!"

Dear Janice and Derek,

I hope this finds you all well and happy. I miss you guys so much! Janice, I can never thank you enough for buying airplane tickets for me and my girls to fly away from Patrick after I divorced him those years ago. And, Derek, I am forever grateful you gave me Frannie the Ford Fairlane to drive when I returned to Tucson. Thank you both so much for taking me in and letting me stay with you on "Sawtelle Spread" when I came back from Orlando to try and get my daughters back. I so enjoyed living with you out there on your 40 acres in the desert. It's a world away from Tucson, isn't it? The desert kinda gets into you, doesn't it? You guys are just pure-tee old desert rats! Guess I am, too, Seattle ain't no desert! But it's nice. And it's gorgeous here once you get used to the damp and chill.

Jerry and I are doing all right. I know you had your doubts about him, especially because we both met in a mental hospital. Wow! What an experience that was! Who could ever have imagined me being catatonic? Thank you so much for your support for me then.

Jerry loves his work with NOAA, but he doesn't like being separated. I kind of enjoy the peace and quiet when he's at sea. I am enjoying my work at the veterinary hospital. It's a small animal hospital so we tend dogs and cats mostly, but Doctor Kurtzmann also sees what are called exotic pets, so we have our share of birds, gerbils, hamsters, and turtles come through the door, too.

My dog, Questra, is wonderful. She will soon be a year old, and is maturing into a very fine-looking dog. The one flop ear gives her an endearingly comical appearance. She's a champ at basic obedience now, and I've taught her a few other things, too. She rides in the passenger seat of the van, one foot on the dashboard, and causes people from other cars to do a double take. Recently, I kinda got myself turned around at Pike Place Market. Ended up nose-to-nose with a Cadillac, and the driver started yelling and shaking his fist at me. I worked the van over as far to the right as I could and we were finally able to get around each other. When he pulled alongside me he was yelling and cursing so loud, Questra decided to step in. She came across the console to my lap from the passenger seat, stuck her big head out my window, and snarled and barked so fierce, he couldn't get away fast enough. Ha-ha. She can look pretty ferocious if she thinks I'm in trouble. I'm glad I have her when I'm alone in the house while Jerry's at sea.

I've learned that this place of constant rain produces amazing flowers. Our house, when we bought it, looked like it was smothered in bushes. We didn't know what they were, and actually thought about pulling them up. Heaven forbid! We now know they are rhododendrons and azaleas, and when they all bloomed, it was pure magic. Hot pink, light pink, white, purplish, so many colors! I did take some pictures but haven't gotten the film developed yet. When I get the pictures, I'll send you some. Right by the front door we have a plum tree, and it blooms in lovely little pink blossoms that become plums if they set. How 'bout that!

How are Sammie and Strawberry doing? I imagine she's about worn out that new saddle on Strawberry by now. He's a good horse. You guys must be very proud of Sammie. She's a fine young girl! I miss her. Please tell her "Aunt Verna" sends her love.

Guys, I can never ever thank you enough for all you did for me when I had my breakdown. The more I get past it, the more I realize just how big of a breakdown it was. All I can say is, I'm really grateful to be past it. I'm still very ashamed that I damaged that window at the Big A Truck Stop. The doctors at Mesquite Valley tell me that was not done consciously, therefore to not blame myself for it, but still, I am deeply mortified at that behavior.

I miss Frannie. The tan Dodge van is a good, dependable vehicle though. And I like being able to sit up so high and have a clear view of traffic. It's a real gas hog, but it sure is a sweet ride.

Next week I'm going to start seeing a new doctor. His name is Doctor Hale. He's a psychiatrist who is available under the insurance Jerry has from NOAA. Doctor Dodd recommended that I continue psychiatric care. Had we stayed in Tucson, I would have continued seeing him on a monthly basis. I'll be sure and let you know how this goes.

Well, it's late, and Questra and I have had a full day, so I'll wind up and say good night. I'll put this in the mail tomorrow.

Love,
Your friend forever, Verna Louise

"How do you do, Doctor Hale. It's nice to meet you." Verna shook hands with her new psychiatrist. His appearance was classic – frizzled graying hair streaked with black, a gray mustache that turned up a little at the corners, glasses on a black cord around his neck, white shirt, collar loose, necktie loosely knotted as if an afterthought, black trousers worn with black suspenders, and glossy black shoes. Her dad always said the appearance of a man's shoes reflected his opinion of himself, so if Doctor Hale was equal to his shoeshine, he must have a large measure of self-esteem.

"Nice to meet you too, Mrs. Hansen. Won't you sit down?" he gestured to an armchair opposite his desk. "Just to get a couple things out of the way before we start…um…do you see the clock there?" He waved a hand vaguely to a clock on a small side table to the right of the room. Present, but not in the line of sight. Verna nodded. "Well, that's a pretty special clock. It's a timer, you see. At twenty-five minutes it will begin to glow. The glow intensifies every ten minutes, until we have reached fifty-five minutes. At fifty-five minutes, it will chime softly. That will mean that our time is up and we must part. But the glow helps keep us on track so we're not suddenly interrupted by the chime. Do you understand?"

Verna glanced at the very ordinary looking clock. "Yes. I've never seen a clock like that."

"My wife gave it to me. It's quite special." He straightened his glasses and folded his hands together in his lap. "I have received your file from Doctor Dodd. Apparently, yours is quite an interesting case."

Interesting case?...Is that all I am to this guy...an interesting case?

"Hmmm...well, I guess a catatonic nurse doesn't come through the door every day, does she?" Verna shifted uncomfortably in her seat. "My goal, Doctor Hale, is that I never have something like that happen to me again. Ever." Verna looked him squarely in the eye. Beyond the veneer of polite civility, there was no room for being fake here. "I hold my mental health at a very high value, having nearly completely lost myself. I've decided it's wise to see you once a month, just as I would see an MD regularly after a severe physical illness." She smiled. "Sort of like taking an extra measure of defense."

He smiled back. "I completely agree, Mrs. Hansen. Let's get started, shall we?"

Questra whelped her puppies as she lay in a large cardboard carton padded with newspapers under the piano in the family room. It was her first litter, and, Verna hoped, her last. First litters were often large. So far, Questra had birthed six puppies. Jerry and Verna sat on the couch watching Julia Child. Verna, pad and pen in her lap frantically wrote down ingredients for a dish called, "Winged Victory." Basically a stuffed chicken breast with the wing still attached.

Julia smiled into the camera, saying, "Dice the carrots very fine, and brown the sliced mushrooms in butter, making sure they are not crowded in the pan."

Another puppy emerged, adding its newborn squeals to the others. "Couldn't she've done that outside in 'er doghouse? I'm tryin' ta watch tv here, an' I don't like that racket." Jerry scowled toward the carton that once held rolls of paper towels. "An' I don't like that smell."

"With your fingers, ease the skin loose from the breast, spoon in your stuffing, and soon you'll be on your way to serving Winged Victory," Julia told them.

"Did she say how many carrots to dice?" Verna asked Jerry.

"How should I know? I can barely hear over these damned puppies!" He rose from the couch, went to the box. and kicked it. "Hush up in there! Hush now!" Questra growled.

Without conscious thought, Verna bolted from the couch, stood between Jerry and the piano, and effectively shielded Questra and the puppies. She placed both palms on his chest and pushed. Gently, but firmly, she pushed him toward the couch. Once he was again seated, she stood in front of him. "Jerry Hansen. Do not ever threaten my dog again. Are you hearing me, Jerry?" She stood and glared at him.

"I thought she'uz *our* dog. It'uz paid fer outta our bank account. That's not *your* dog, it's *our* dog." He frowned but didn't stand up.

"Do you want your money back?" Verna had hands on hips now, pad, pen, and recipe forgotten. "Questra is here when you are away. She is very protective of me. I trained her. She trusts me."

A new squeal sounded from the whelping box.

"Well, it's *my* piano. Take *your* dog outta from under *my* piano. Put 'er damn box outside."

"Jerry, I will do no such thing. The doghouse roof leaks. It's forty-five degrees outside. She is *giving birth*. She needs to be inside where it's warm with her puppies. She's best out of the way under the piano. When the puppies are older, then we can repair the doghouse, and they can live there until they're six weeks old when I will take them to Frau Frisch. She will pay me a percentage of the puppies' sale. Tell you what. I will give you all the money from the puppies' sale. *All of it!* These puppies, because of their bloodline, are priced at one hundred fifty dollars each with their AKC papers. She already has people on waiting lists at her kennels. There is no doubt they will sell. Don't say another word about Questra going outside to whelp in the rain."

"This is Julia Child...Bon Appetit!" Julia's show was over.

Verna's show with Jerry still had some playing time left before it ended.

Questra whelped nine live puppies. The tenth, a male, was stillborn. Verna carefully buried him in the back yard, bringing to mind a funeral she held for a dead kitten years ago when she taught her daughters about death. The kitten's name was Tom. In his memory, Verna named the puppy "TomToo." Being stillborn, he had already crossed The Rainbow Bridge, but Verna felt his spirit should know who he could have been. Perhaps he would meet KittenTom over The Rainbow Bridge. Perhaps KittenTom would tell TomToo of Verna's gentle, loving care she gave him before his passing, and perhaps that could help TomToo's spirit be at ease. Verna hoped so. Surely God, in His Loving Wisdom, had a special place for animals in His Heaven. Verna loved animals, and one of her favorite Scriptures was Job 12: 7-10, *"But ask now the beasts, and they shall teach thee; and the fowls of the air, and they shall tell thee. Or speak to the earth, and it shall teach thee; and the fishes of the sea shall declare until thee. Who knoweth not in all these that the hand of the Lord hath wrought this? In whose hand is the soul of every living thing, and the breath of all mankind."* And so she blessed the lifeless puppy, now "TomToo," gently laid him in his grave, and returned him to the earth. Later she planted a dogwood tree next to the burial spot in his honor. TomToo's memory would live in the tree and its white blossoms that opened every spring.

Questra continued a low growl whenever Jerry was nearby. Verna repaired the doghouse, making it snug and dry. Then she moved Questra and the puppies there when their eyes opened. When the pups were six weeks old, she took them to Frau Frisch who wrote her a generous check. Verna drove home, endorsed the check, and gave it to Jerry without another word. The entire experience had given her much more than merely a "glimpse" of that mental patient she once met in Mesquite Valley Mental Hospital!

"So, I've come to the conclusion that he just doesn't like babies. People babies. Animal babies. Any babies. Jerry just doesn't seem to have any kind of a nurturing gene in him. He is just...well...he is Jerry." Verna looked bleakly at Doctor Hale who sat behind his desk, his hands folded on his small paunch.

"What did he expect to happen when he kicked the box?" Doctor Hale unwrapped a mint chocolate and popped it in his mouth. He shoved the dish in Verna's direction, and she shook her head.

"Well, I guess he expected Questra to somehow quiet the puppies. I mean, heck, they weren't loud for heaven's sake…they were just newly born and squealing with their first breaths." Verna reached for the candy dish after all, took a chocolate, and began to unwrap it slowly.

"He wanted to assert authority over his house," said Doctor Hale. "I rather doubt he had any real authority over his ex and his children." He swallowed the chocolate. "Did he have a dog as a child? Any pets?"

"No. He grew up under his grandmother's care, and she was raising four boys alone on practically no money from what I've heard. There was no money for pet expenses. Jerry grew up constantly hearing how terrible everything was, how expensive everything was, and wearing the other boys' hand-me-downs. He rarely even got a new pair of shoes. Sad." Verna shook her head at the situation as the chocolate melted in her mouth.

The timer clock was glowing brightly. It would chime shortly. "So, Verna, to wrap up today, you need to ask yourself, one, do you love the man, and two, could you be happy on your own without him. I rather seriously doubt your husband has the capacity to love that you have, and I seriously doubt you will ever have what you really need from him." The clock chimed softly, and Doctor Hale stood.

"But I don't want to get divorced again," Verna said as she rose. "I really don't. I meant my marriage vows, even if they were said in a little chapel in Las Vegas." She sighed. She'd learned that Doctor Hale rarely said anything once the clock chimed.

As he opened the door to usher her out, he said, "Then you will learn to live in a loveless marriage, my dear."

Oh, dear God, what have I done? Again! Oh, Father, please help me! Please show me the way! Please show me a sign! If this is one of Your "Mysterious Ways," please show me the Wonder in it soon!

Verna would see the Wonder; she would marvel at it, be immersed in it, thank God daily for it. But its time was not yet.

Jerry submitted an application to work at Seattle's Air National Guard complex. He decided he didn't want to be separated from Verna for weeks at a time. They were on a short vacation while he was waiting to hear if he was to be interviewed. The ferry ride on Puget Sound was heavenly. A small boy flew a kite from the stern, and some passengers threw bread up at the seagulls hovering in the wind. Verna bought a coffee and a cinnamon roll and handed it to Jerry to take a bite.

"Wow. That's tha best cinnamon roll I ever ate. Yum yum for tha tum tum," said Jerry with a smile. Verna was glad to see it. There had been a chill between them since the day he kicked Questra's box.

"Just wait til you try the coffee. It's nearly as good as Starbucks'." Verna handed him the cup. He drank deeply.

"Well, it's good, but it's no Starbucks. It's good an' hot, though." He handed the cup back. "So, I think it'll be better ta work on land an' not be goin' out ta sea alla time. I'll be home for dinner ever' night. We can go ta church together ever' Sunday." He shrugged. "They barely even know me at our church."

"The important thing, Jerry, is that you be happy in your work. You earned your position on that ship. Would you be happy working at the Air National Guard?" Verna looked at him earnestly.

"I think I'll be happy if I can be with you ever' night," he said and put his arm around her. A seagull defecated on the shoulder of his parka.

Uh…hmmm…one of the signs I asked for?

"Thank you for spaying Questra, Doctor Griffin. She surely made beautiful puppies, but I don't want to have to worry about her getting bred again. No more puppies for us." Verna laid her still sleeping dog on a towel in a kennel with a drape in front so she could wake up peacefully.

"You're welcome, Verna." The vet stood and looked at his assistant for a moment. He'd never had anyone in his employ like her. She had a real gift with the animals, and she applied all of her surgical training in assisting him and his associate with procedures. She was also great with pet owners. Often owners needed coddling while their animals pretty much took things in stride.

She latched the kennel and turned to go. He put his hand on her shoulder. "Verna, are you happy here? I'm sure you don't get the challenges here that you would have in a hospital operating room." His brown eyes were gentle, searching.

"Yes. I am, Doctor Griffin. I told you. I like the work. I've missed it." She turned again to go, and again he restrained her with a hand on her shoulder.

"Then what is it? You are obviously unhappy about something, and I just assumed it was because you worked here instead of in your true field." He waited.

She sighed. "Well...you know the old saying, 'Marry in haste, repent at leisure?' I've twice now married in haste." She took a deep breath, and it all tumbled out. "I thought I loved my husband. I did. Really. But, now I see I don't even know him. He has...for want of a better word, temper tantrums. I never know from one moment to the next what he's going to do. Or say. He says the most hurtful things sometimes." She heard her name being called from the reception area. Thanks to her suggestion, they had hired an office manager, but she had no background in veterinary practice so was constantly asking for help. "Thanks, Doctor Griffin, but I really love being here."

Verna put the last ornament on the small evergreen tree in the family room. Their previous Christmas was a non-event since they had barely arrived in Seattle and dealt with all the disappointments in the rental house. Verna was determined to make Christmas 1977 nice for them. Jerry's gifts from his children were under the tree. He had sent them each a check for ten dollars. Verna bought him a leather briefcase and a pen that wrote from all angles and even under water. The atmosphere between them had somewhat improved since he'd gone to work at the Guard. They'd taken a vacation to Port Townsend, and had finally spent an evening dining at the Space Needle's revolving restaurant. Earlier this day, she'd taken the van to the carwash, cleaned it thoroughly, and applied air freshener liberally. He often complained it smelled of dog, with dog hair embedded in its carpet.

"Merry Christmas, Jerry," she said as he entered the house. The lights on the tree glowed softly in the dusk, and classic Christmas music floated in the air. The Christmas ham, studded with cloves and pineapple rings, roasted in the oven, and the house smelled like the holiday.

He made a nondescript sound that sounded something like "Go to hell." Verna followed him to the bedroom where he would change. "What did you just say?" She stood in the doorway hoping she had misunderstood.

He whirled at her from the closet. "I said go to Hell." He unbuttoned his shirt and prepared to take it off.

Tears threatened, but Verna was determined not to cry. Doctor Hale reiterated that communication was the real basis for a sound marriage. "Jerry Hansen, I do not deserve that. Why do you say such a thing?"

"Oh, I think you know why," he snarled. "I saw the bank statement. Been pretty spendy haven't you?" He unzipped his trousers and sat on the bed to untie his shoes.

"Spendy?" Verna thought a moment. "Do you mean the gifts I sent my mother and her husband? The gifts I sent to Janice and Derek? I made handmade gifts, and all they cost was the postage. Surely you don't mean postage!"

He removed his wallet and took out a folded piece of paper. "What's this?" He flung it at her.

As she read it she began to almost giggle. "This? This is the receipt for the gift I bought for you!" She stood there, arms at her sides. Verna had learned the importance of body language, so purposely did not fold her arms over her bosom. "We agreed to buy each other one gift, did we not?"

Jerry paused in his furious undressing, brow furrowed. "Well...uh...yes. Yes, we did." He looked up at her from the bed.

"I bought you a gift. Actually, two. And I sent gifts and cards, from us, to the children. Handmade. Didn't cost a dime. I bought the tree, lights, and ornaments simply because we didn't have any. That, dear Jerry, is not *spendy*. That is Christmas." Tears started to fall now, so she turned and went to the kitchen to check on the ham.

Questra lay quietly under the piano in the family room. It was her favorite place in the house. She could smell her puppies there. Hearing Jerry's voice, a low growl simmered in her chest.

THE SEATTLE TIMES

Verna and Jerry earnestly began shopping for a new house in the new year, 1978. They decided their relationship's "main problem" was their present house. True, it was small and at the end of a dead end street near I-5 with constant freeway noise which Verna tuned out long ago. To her, it sounded like a rushing river – except for the occasional siren. Or crash. Jerry decided he must have a view. Water, perhaps, or mountains. No longer at sea for weeks at a time, he grew bored with only the piano, television, and his daily run for diversion. Now, after viewing numerous houses for sale as they had before buying this one, their next option was building. They sat at the kitchen table, poring over brochures and builders' pamphlets.

"I really don't want a split-level, Jerry. As I've told you, I don't want to deal with stairs. I prefer ranch-style. All one level." Verna leaned back in her chair, picked up her coffee, sipped, made a face, and set it down. It was cold.

"Verna, I'm not even real sure we can afford to do *this*." He gestured at a pamphlet. "Of all the plans this builder offers, this is the least expensive. Apparently, he builds many of this particular model." He studied Verna over his coffee cup. She could be so stubborn! "There are other models, but they cost more to build. It's either this or stay here in this miserably tiny house." He gestured around. "I mean, look at this place. Where will we put the boys when they come for their visit this summer, huh? I only just got Mary Ann to agree to it, so now I'll be bringing them to this?" He went to the sink and tossed his cold coffee down the drain. "Unless you can figure out a way for us to have more income than we do now so we can afford a more costly model, this is our choice." He turned to her, leaning his back against the sink. "You could see about going to work in a real hospital, maybe? How much would you make as an LPN doing patient care? Do you even know? I mean, you kinda jumped in at the veterinary clinic, didn't you? Because you were too stubborn to accept another position in a hospital?"

Verna turned in her seat and regarded him. "I am an OR nurse, Jerry. Yes, I'm an LPN, but I want to work in the OR. That's not done here. Nobody will even review my credentials. I make the same working for Doctor Griffin here as I did in the OR at Saint Joe's in Tucson. I love the work. I love the animals. I have Sundays off. No call. No nights. I'm at home in veterinary medicine."

Jerry yanked his keys off the hook and headed for the door. "Well, then. Why don't you just take your damn dog and go live *there*!" He grabbed his parka and went out. Gravel from the driveway peppered the side of the house as he angrily sped away.

Verna sighed. Too many of their conversations became arguments, and arguments always seemed to end with Jerry stomping out the door and driving away.

"Mrs. Hansen, the problem is not the house. It never is. Couples in trouble usually try one or all three of these options – buy a house, buy a car, or have a baby." He peered at her over his spectacles. "I gather from your medical history you will not be having a baby? Yes?" Verna nodded. "So, here you are, trying to buy a house. Believe me when I tell you, living in a different house is not going to make living together any easier." He nudged the candy dish toward her. Today, pastel jelly beans. She took a pink one and looked at Doctor Hale. He saw the pain in her eyes. The clock chimed its single chime, and he stood. "Mrs. Hansen, there are options other than trying to build a house on which neither of you can agree. Perhaps you should think on those a bit." He walked around the desk and opened the door.

"Thank you, Doctor Hale. Bye." Verna, donning her new rust-colored Gore-Tex parka, headed for the elevator. A water-resistant parka was of primary importance. As always, Jerry balked at the cost, but eventually they each bought one of good quality during after-Christmas sales. She zipped it closed as she headed for the van. Questra saw her through the windshield and barked joyously.

"I'm glad to see you too, Girl. Where shall we go, huh? Wanna go to the park? Huh? We could go to the park and you could chase the ball?" Questra wagged, barked, and danced. Verna loved her dog. The van, which needed a tune-up, started on the third try, and she backed confidently out of the big parking lot.

One thing I've learned to do really well is drive this van...

She stopped at a Starbucks drive-through for coffee and saw a newspaper on the counter next to the cashier. "You through with The Times?" she asked. The lady nodded, smiled, and passed her the paper and hot coffee, both welcome.

The day was cold and gray, misty droplets floating in a foggy soup. After playing ball with Questra for an hour, Verna sat on a bench in the park, Questra curled up next to her, tail tucked over her nose. Verna opened the paper to look for the crossword puzzle when a quarter-page ad caught her eye.

"Drivers Wanted – Must have one ton van, current Washington State driver's license, excellent driving record, and insurance. Pay is $9.50 an hour plus mileage driving for the Seattle Times. Must pass test. Will train." Verna put the paper down, an idea blossoming. *Hmm...nine-fifty an hour plus mileage...more money than I'm making now, that's for sure...maybe if I made more money, that would shut Jerry up...would hate to leave the vet clinic, but...more money?... can't hurt to apply, at least...*

Questra, Verna was certain, could read her thoughts, for she sat up and began wagging her tail. "You think it's a good idea too, don't you, Girl?" Questra woofed in agreement, jumped down off the bench, and invited Verna to follow her to the van.

"Ned, I'm tellin' ya, we have ta at least interview women. Give'm tha test. It's this whole Equal Employment Opportunity thing. It's like...a law...er sump'n... gotta give women an *opportunity* ta git a man's job...it's tha damndest thing..." Jack Kelly sighed in disgust, lit a cigarette, and looked at Ned Flatt. He could see his mind working.

"Well, sure, we gotta give'm tha test. But...if they can't do tha work, then we don't have ta hire'm. This is a man's job, after all. Takes considerable strength ta manage tha bundles, an' they gotta read tha maps so's they can find tha addresses okay, an' ya know how screwed up some-a them suburbs are. Most places there ain't even a real grid, it jus' all...winds around." Ned drummed his fingers on his oak desk. "How many've applied so far today?"

"Twenty eight men, an' it's just after twelve." Jack glanced up at the ancient clock on the wall. Ned Flatt had inherited a very old office on the top floor of the Seattle Times downtown corporate offices. The clock was probably older than both of them. It had to be wound at the beginning of every day with a large brass key.

"Any of'm women?" Ned squinted as the cigarette smoke reached his eyes and flapped a hand in annoyance. He'd quit cigarettes three years earlier.

Jack shrugged. "I dunno. I'll go by Personnel an' see. Jus' figgered they'uz all men, y'know? Thought I'd head over ta tha warehouse an' take a look at tha applicants gettin' ready ta do tha test. Wanna come?" Ned stood and shrugged into his brown tweed jacket. He was a very big man with very wide shoulders. All his suits and jackets were tailor made. Hair graying at the temples and dark eyes under beetling brows gave him an almost "movie star tough guy" appearance which he used to his advantage to intimidate when he felt necessary. He had the same gym equipment in his home that was available to professional football players and worked on his physique daily.

As they stepped into a massive, echoing room with a buffed cement floor, they could hear the constant rumble of machinery bearing miles of newspapers on conveyor belts over their heads. A large group of men milled about on one side, murmuring to each other. In the middle of the cement expanse a man walked with a bundle of newspapers in each hand. A voice called out, "You'll have ta show more hustle than that if ya want this job!" The man hurried faster, dropped the bundles at the far side of the room, turned, and looked back. The voice called out, "Okay, now bring 'em back, an' ya better show more hustle. We're a newspaper, fer Chris'sake! Iz all 'bout deadlines. C'mon now. Move!" The man bent, picked up the bundles, hefted them for a moment, dropped them back on the floor, shook his head, held up both hands in mock surrender, and walked out a side door into the parking lot. The voice yelled, "Next!"

"Hi, there. I'm Verna Hansen. I just saw this ad in the paper. Where do I apply?" She stood in front of the reception desk at Seattle Times Corporate with the paper in her hand. She'd never been in a newspaper office before and found the bustle of it fascinating. The receptionist, whose desk name plate identified her as "Joyce K. Editor of First Impressions," looked up and squinted slightly. "Which ad? Which job?" Verna laid the paper on the desk, touched the ad with her finger, and slid it towards her. "This job." Verna waited. Joyce stood and smiled. "Right this way, Mrs...Hansen? Did you say?" Verna nodded and followed the young, smartly-dressed-in-a-cranberry-skirt-and-jacket-suit-and-shiny-black-high-heels, shoulder-length-blonde-haired woman as her heels click-clacked out a side door, pleated skirt swaying as she went.

In the loading dock area the "Editor of First Impressions" walked up to a very tall man in a tweed jacket and said, "Mr. Flatt, this is Mrs. Hansen. She is here to apply." She turned to Verna. "This is Mr. Flatt. He's Vice President of Circulation." Joyce turned and left to a chorus of appreciative wolf whistles and "Look at that skirt swing, won'tcha?" as she clattered across the cement floor. Head high, she ignored them.

Verna reached automatically to shake hands and was astonished at the size of the hand that engulfed hers. Dark eyes pleasantly looked her over, as another man carried two newspaper bundles across the expanse of cement, set them down, picked them up, and hurried back. He was panting slightly as he set them down near Verna and rejoined the group of milling applicants.

"How do you do, Mrs. Hansen." Ned Flatt released her hand and nodded slightly to the man who had been calling out for people to carry the newspapers. "Nelson, give Mrs. Hansen here tha test."

Barry Nelson, a middle-aged, balding man, approached Verna with an oddly aggressive posture, hands on hips. "My name's Mr. Nelson. Ya ever worked atta newspaper before?" he barked. Verna shook her head. He sighed, shoulders slumped dramatically, as if she were wasting his time. "Aw right, then. See, what we're all about here is circulation. That means papers come offa tha press," he gestured to the end of the conveyor belts where the papers were stacked, bundled with plastic straps, and loaded by hand onto wooden pallets. "They leave this dock in big trucks ta be taken ta distribution warehouses alla 'roun' tha city. There them bundles're loaded inta vans an' taken to tha homes-a carriers, an' they takes tha papers direct ta customers. Got it?" Verna nodded. "So...ta do this job, ya gotta know how ta handle bundles. Lots an' lotsa bundles." He grinned a flippant, demeaning, scornful grin at her in challenge. "Think ya can handle it, sweetheart?" he sneered.

Something bristly reared its head inside Verna – something that arched its back, flattened its ears, stood its hair straight up, narrowed its eyes, and rumbled deep inside. The man had obviously already dismissed her as being incapable.

"Yep. I think I can."

She looked down at the bundles on the floor, looked up at Mr. Flatt, batted her eyes, smiled a girlishly-sweet smile at Barry Nelson, and said, "So, to be clear, the point of this exercise is to pick up these two bundles and take them over there." She pointed across the room. "Drop them on the floor, pick them up, and bring them back?" She looked from one man to the other. The group of men milling about stilled and focused its interest on her. The murmur quieted. Now the only sound in the massive room was the rumble of the machinery. Nelson and Flatt nodded.

"Ya got it. 'at's tha point of it, little lady." Barry Nelson pompously pronounced. "Pick'm up, take'm over, drop'm, pick'm up, bring'm back, 'an drop'm. Quick."

Jack Kelly lit another cigarette.

As Verna bent to slip her hands under the straps, a man shouted, "Careful of yer manicure, darlin'." She ignored it, gazed across the fifty-foot expanse of gray cement, picked up two bundles, and moved quickly, a bundle in each hand, to the other side of the room. The paper bundles were heavy, certainly – she would learn they weighed forty pounds each – but she had hefted dogs that were heavier at veterinary hospitals. She had lifted patients in and out of chairs and beds as a nurse. As a teenager she had unloaded hundred-pound feed sacks, carried them up ladders, and stacked them in the barn loft for the horses. Now she walked briskly across the room, set the two bundles down, flexed her fingers, picked them up again and rapidly returned, plopping the bundles down at the feet of the man who had sneered at her. He stood silently, slack-jawed.

"You mean like that, Mr. Nelson?"

"Do you have a van, Mrs. Hansen?" asked Mr. Flatt. "If you do, what kind is it?"

"It's a one ton Dodge van. My husband and I moved here from Arizona in it two years ago."

"Can you drive it?"

"Yes. In fact, I drove it here. Would you like to see it?"

Ned Flatt, Jack Kelly, and Verna proceeded to the parking lot. Questra waited expectantly in the passenger seat. She doggy grinned at them, her one flop ear making her appear a canine comedienne, and woofed once in greeting. She hopped over the console to the driver's side and poked her wet, black nose out the open space at the top of the window.

"That's my van, right there." Verna gestured, and the two men paused at sight of the big dog. Questra weighed about one hundred twenty five pounds. A formidable size.

Verna approached the side of the van with her key. Unlocking the doors she said, "Questra. Down. Stay." Obediently, the dog dropped to her belly on the carpeted floor and regarded the two men with interest.

"Is that dog gonna bite us?" asked Jack.

"No, sir. Questra will only do what I tell her to do. Trained her myself." At the sound of her name, Questra's tail thumped the carpeted floor, but she stayed where she was. Both men peered inside the van. Since they'd arrived in Seattle, Jerry had installed insulation, paneling, and a carpeted headliner inside the van, converting it into a camper. They still had not gone camping, but it was a very inviting looking vehicle, nicely finished inside. Jack whistled appreciatively.

"You do all 'is yaself?"

"My husband, Jerry, and I worked on it together. The bed comes out, though, so the entire space is available to haul newspaper bundles." She patted Questra's head and said, "Good girl."

Ned and Jack looked at each other. Jack said, "Well, thanks for coming by. We'll check out your driving record, and schedule your vehicle maintenance test, but you look like a...well...a pretty good candidate for the job." Jack looked pleasant enough, but, to Verna, he still looked stand-offish somehow, as if not convinced a woman could do this job.

"Vehicle maintenance test?"

"Well, of course. All candidates for this position have to demonstrate they can...you know...check their oil...change a tire...put on chains...you know...basic vehicle maintenance. We'll give you a call." Mr. Flatt shook Verna's hand, and she shut the side doors.

The bristly thing that had awakened inside Verna now set its jaw firmly, crossed its arms, and sat down solidly within her. She decided she would get this job and do this work just to show them she could.

"You're going to *what*? What didju say you're goin' ta tha Community College for? I don't unnerstand." Jerry stood in the living room, looking per-plexed. "Why do ya need ta take a course in vehicle maintenance? You gonna be a mechanic now?"

"No, not a mechanic. A driver. For the Seattle Times. I have to be able to demonstrate that I can do basic vehicle maintenance. Just simple things really... like change oil, change a tire, put on chains. You know...just some basic stuff." She poured him some coffee and set it on the kitchen table. "Come on over and sit down. The course is four weeks, Monday, Wednesday, and Friday nights from seven to nine." She added cream to her coffee, along with a squirt of honey, and stirred.

He sat, slurped his coffee, and regarded his wife. "You. A driver. With our van." Absently he picked up his coffee cup. "Jus' where wouldja drive it to? Huh? They tell you that part?"

"Well, I'll drive it wherever they say, I suppose. It will be in King County, though, I'm pretty sure. Questra can go with me." Verna smiled. Hearing her name, Questra came to Verna and laid her head in her lap. Verna rubbed her dog's ears affectionately and drank her coffee. "I'll be paid nine dollars and fifty cents an hour, plus mileage. It will be more money coming in. More than I would make if I were to go to work in patient care, that's for sure." She didn't say anything about the bristly thing that was suddenly awake and standing on its hind legs inside her.

Jerry drank his coffee. "More money, huh? Oh…Well…uh…Do we have any cookies?"

"Yes, right over there, Miz..uh...Hansen is it? That right?" Gary Lawson glanced at the clipboard in his hand, then gestured to a row of hooks on the wall. "Jus' hang yer coat up, an' I'll give ya tha gran' tour." Lawson was old school. He believed firmly in his heart that God did not intend for women to do men's work. Women belonged at home, making excellent meals, keeping a tidy house, and, most of all, remaining available to their families, especially their husbands. He scowled at her back as she turned away to remove her coat.

"This is a pallet jack." He pointed at an orange metal device with a tall handle, two protruding prongs, and two close-set wheels. "Ya roll it unner a pallet-a newspapers like this, see?" He demonstrated. "Then you, all by yerself, kin move 'at heavy pallet anywheres ya need it ta be." He released the lever and lowered the pallet. "You try."

Verna pumped the pallet of newspaper bundles up on the jack, pulled the handle, and wheeled the pallet over to another pallet of newspapers. She lowered it and removed the jack. "Like that?" She smiled her most winning smile.

"Yeah. Jus' like that." Hearing a motor approaching, he said, "Come on over ta tha dock. Truck's here. You kin unload 'er." The huge door of the loading bay raised, letting in a blast of chilly air, and a big truck backed up to it. A man got a pallet jack, tucked it underneath an empty wooden pallet, and rolled it over to the dock just as the truck driver raised the back door of his heavily loaded truck. It was stacked to the top with newspaper bundles. The driver tossed bundles to two men standing on the loading dock, who started to stack them on the pallet.

"Move outta tha way, guys. Miz Hansen here's gonna unload this truck. Ain'tcha, Sweetie?" Gary grinned, folded his arms, and leaned against a Masonite-topped work counter. The other men joined him and also leaned casually to watch, all smirking at this upstart woman who thought she was going to do a man's job. The driver looked at them and frowned. "What's 'is? Hey! You know it takes two stackers ta unload my truck! Come on!" He stood in the opening, big hand resting on a stack of bundles. "I said, I ain't movin' til ya's git 'nother spotter over here." Gary nodded to one of the men. "Go on over there an' help tha lady, Paulie."

Verna on one side of the pallet and Paulie on the other caught the bundles and stacked them in a crisscrossing pattern, called, "tying the stack." It made the bundles more stable and easier to move. Verna learned quickly and matched the driver's rhythm so the job flowed smoothly. She was sweating by the time the pallet was full. Another man pumped up the jack and moved it out of the way as Verna pumped another jack under an empty pallet and brought it over. One of the first things she learned working in the OR was to anticipate what was needed and make it ready. She also observed the men rotated their positions, with two stacking bundles and a third maneuvering the jack. Then he would move to the front and stack bundles, while one of the front men moved to the jack.

Like playing volleyball...everyone plays their position then rotates...hmmm...

Finally the big truck was empty, and the filled pallets of bundled newspapers lined the warehouse walls. The driver rolled his back door down, jumped down, and snugged it tight. He saluted the crew, wiped his sweaty face, returned to the cab of his truck, and drove away with a grinding of gears. Gary took a clipboard down from the wall and jerked his chin at Verna. "I'll give ya an easy run t'day, seein' as yer new." He handed her the clipboard. "This here's Hawthorne. Go getcher truck an' let's loadja up." He glanced around at the other men. "Paulie, you go on out with 'er an' show 'er how ta spot papers."

"Why in tha world would Gary startcha on Hawthorne? It's one-a tha toughest runs we have. All hills. Seattle's like Rome, y'know. Built on seven hills. Maybe more." Paulie gestured at the intersection for Verna to turn right. He held up the clipboard and showed her the address in the left column, the carrier's name in the middle, and the newspaper count on the right. Verna scanned the street addresses as she drove. Paulie was the youngest man at the Lake City Warehouse. He wore his blonde hair long and apparently was trying to grow a mustache; his upper lip looked shadowy.

"There tis, ma'am. Right there. See tha porch? We s'posed ta spot tha papers onna porch right next ta tha door."

"*Spot* the papers?"

"Yes'm. Place'm. Put'm down where they's suppos'd ta go inna same spot ever' time so's tha carriers kin git'm easy. Carriers kin be right pertic'ler where they wants their papers, so we makes little notes next ta their names. See?" He showed her the note on the clipboard and indicated each name on the list. Most had a notation next to them. "We *spots* tha papers fer tha carriers. 'at's why we's called spotters...'cause we spot."

Like surgeons...they each want something unique to them...interesting...

As she drove that day, all her senses were on hypervigilant alert. She had to watch traffic, pay attention to what her guide was telling her, lift heavy bundles, carry them to the exact designated spot, and, in most cases, bag them with plastic bags due to damp rainy weather so common it was just a part of life. The plastic straps on the bundles had sharp edges, and her hands became painfully shredded. Paulie noticed and said, "Geez...din't nobody tell ya? Ya gotta tape yer hands." He turned his own over, indicating strips of white adhesive tape protectively wrapped around his fingers. He reached in his pocket and removed an odd fingerless glove and gave it to her. "Here. Put this'n on. I wish I'd knowedja weren't done up proper. I'da helpedcha with that."

The glove did help. By the time she returned home, though, after driving four runs, her hands were a bloody mess. She soaked them in ice water, determined to make a go of this new job. She was in a whole new world. A world of hard working men in a blue collar environment. Most of them resented her greatly. One said multiple times he had six kids and needed the job. She, in his opinion, had a husband to provide for her. Thus she was taking a job away from a man who needed it to support a family. Paulie became a wealth of information. He and his older sister were orphaned young, so she basically raised him, as well as worked to support the two of them. He admired a woman who wanted to work as hard as a man, so he helped Verna all he could.

Paulie's admiration was well founded, for Verna did work as hard as a man – even harder because she, as the first woman to work on a Seattle Times loading dock, had to overcome stereotype as well as flagrant prejudice and chauvinism from men in whose midst she worked. It was hard enough being treated as an "uppity woman who didn't know her place" or as a sexual conquest by guys who felt they were God's gift to women. Plus she stepped into a murderous, mind-numbing work schedule, the only "saving grace" being she and all her "fellow spotters" followed the same schedule. The Times was an evening paper during the week, carrier-delivered every afternoon Monday through Friday; on Saturday and Sunday it was delivered in the morning. Therefore, a "spotter's schedule" was:

Monday through Thursday – 11:00am – 4:00pm
Friday – 11:00am – 4:00pm *and* 12:00midnight – 7:00am for Saturday
      morning delivery
Saturday – 12:00midnight – 7:00am for Sunday morning delivery
Sunday – 7:00am off until Monday at 11:00am

Days off rotated every week until there was a weekend off every six weeks.

These hours, of course, did not count the ones traveling to and from work, nor did these "posted schedules" account for late trucks from Central Publishing or unavoidable delays. It was work in all weathers, fair and foul. Hard, tiring, muscle-aching work it was, a challenge most certainly, but a challenge Verna rose to face, conquer, and command with pride in the overcoming of it. She would do this for nine years – years in which she grew into herself.

WHAT DID YOU SAY?

Verna slept fitfully and fell into a dream. She was outdoors following Veronica. Her eldest daughter, glancing over her shoulder periodically, scrambled over rocks and gravel and brush, apparently in the desert. She was panting slightly for she'd been running. Verna could actually feel her heart thumping. There was something black under a bush ahead of her. A backpack. Veronica picked it up and put her arms through the straps. As she straightened up to run again, Verna's phone rang.

"Verna, listen to me. Tell me the truth. Is she there with you?" Anne Marie's shrill voice sounded fretful, frightened, agitated, angry, and tearfully worried.

"Excuse me? Anne Marie? Is *who* here with me?" Verna, foggy with sleep, had just barely started dreaming. The ringing phone shattered the dream into shards of images – sand, brush, gravel, something black. She raised up on her elbows to listen better.

"Veronica!" Anne Marie screamed into the phone. "Your oldest daughter! She's gone. We think she might be trying to find you." Anne Marie's voice broke. "She...she's run away."

Verna jerked upright. "What did you say? Veronica? Run away?" She turned back the covers and stood. Questra, instantly at her feet, alert, looked up at her, sensing something was very wrong. "How? What? Who?? Verna forced herself to take a deep breath. "Just calm down, Anne Marie, and tell me what's happened." Verna automatically shifted into "Nurse Mode," so she sounded calm, reasonable, even professional.

"She didn't come home from school yesterday. Mother called me at work to tell me she was not on the bus and hadn't come home. I called the school and they said she hadn't been there. There was a mix-up about whether to call me or Patrick, so no one called. We've been searching and calling people here, and we can't find her. Patrick thinks she's run away and that she's probably trying to get to you somehow." Anne Marie was near her limit of coherence.

As the awful truth of the words penetrated, Verna's mind exploded with a million panicky possibilities. "Stay on the line, Anne Marie, I'm going to the other phone." She laid the receiver on the nightstand, ran to the kitchen table, and picked up the other phone. "Now. You tell me she got on the bus as usual yesterday, went to school you thought, only wasn't actually in school? And she didn't come home?" Verna's breath came in short, panting, gasps.

"There was a substitute teacher for her class, so they...they..." Anne Marie's voice trailed off into sobs, and Patrick came on the line.

"Verna Louise, you tell me right now if my daughter is there with you!' he growled. Verna heard the *clink* of the Zippo lighter and Patrick's intake as he took the first drag off a cigarette.

"Patrick, no one is here but me. Jerry has gone to work. I worked last night from midnight till eight this morning and just got to sleep when the phone rang." She paused for breath. "Have you called the police? Have you reported her missing? What if she was kidnapped? What if she's hurt somewhere? Have you called her grandparents? My mother in Florida?" Verna's thoughts scrambled over possibilities like spiders over a wall.

Veronica...gone...missing...my eldest daughter...disappeared...

"Patrick! How did you let this happen?" Verna paced as much as the length of the telephone cord would allow, Questra matching step for step, whimpering quietly in sympathy.

"'Course we called the police. Last night. An' the hospitals. So she isn't there, huh?" Patrick stilled for a moment. "Good idea about the grandparents. I'll call 'em. Bye. Oh. Just a minute. If you hear from her, you call us right away! We'll come get her!" He hung up.

Wide awake now, no possibility of sleep, Verna dressed in jeans and sweatshirt, finally acclimated enough to the Pacific Northwest that she'd packed away her red fleece long-johns. Her mind cast wildly to and fro in panic. She wanted to run in all directions at once. She wanted to get Susanna and bring her home. Keep her safe. Without permission from her, her body sank down on a chair, wracked with sobs. She was nearly emotionally destroyed. She felt certain her interrupted dream was Veronica leaving.

Oh, Dear God, keep her safe!...Wherever she is, please keep my eldest daughter safe!

Tucson police conducted an intensive search for several days. It was learned she had not boarded the school bus the morning she disappeared. Patrick and Anne Marie felt she was still in their area, so he drove miles through Tucson hoping to glimpse her. They called the morgue for information on any "Jane Does" of the same age and size, and went once to see if one was Veronica. Thank God she was not.

Days wore into weeks, and weeks wore into months with no word. Verna was numb with woe. Jerry, concerned for her mental health, arranged to accompany her to her psychiatric appointment.

As she exited the inner sanctum, Jerry put down his magazine and stood to walk out with her. "Well? What did he say? Are you all right?" He took her arm and they proceeded to the elevator.

"Yes, I'm all right." She looked at him as they stepped in. "I'm not going catatonic any time soon, if that's what you mean." Verna pushed the lobby button.

"Jerry, I only want one thing. I want my daughter to be okay. If she, by some miracle, makes it here to Washington State and finds us, then we will welcome her, do you understand me?" The bell dinged, and they stepped off the elevator. Jerry didn't speak, but he nodded. Questra awaited them in the van, her nose pressed against the opening at the top of the window on the passenger side. She woofed at sight of Verna. Verna's heart eased a bit.

Veronica, only thirteen years old, left home with nothing but the clothes she was wearing and a comb in her pocket. Her savings account at the bank hadn't been touched. Her Barbie backpack was found under a bush in the park, sans lunch box and thermos. The one Verna saw her pick up in her dream was black. She knew in her heart her daughter decided to run away. She also knew in her heart her eldest was an extremely self-reliant little girl, with a great deal more intelligence than for which she was given credit. Verna never felt she was in true danger, and never felt she was anything but alive. Yet the concern for Veronica joined the fretfulness for Susanna and the sadness for Chrissy; Verna gathered them all in a "Bother Ball," wrapped it in "Prayer Paper," tied it with "Trust Twine," and stored it in a deep part of her being. There would come a day when that package was unwrapped and its contents released in joy restored.

Life's rhythms resumed. Jerry rode with his carpool to his office at the Air National Guard. Verna drove the tan Dodge van to the Lake City Distribution Center every day, radio playing country music, Questra sitting upright in the passenger seat, one paw on the dash. Verna learned well, much to the men's surprise. Her delivery runs were completed on time; she didn't complain and mostly kept to herself. As her hands had callused over and toughened up, so had she.

One dark and rainy night Verna pulled up to the curb of a city park. The bundles for this carrier were to be spotted precisely at the base of a certain streetlight. She stood facing the side of the van as she counted, bagged, and prepared to drop them there. Questra usually sat quietly in the passenger seat. Now, though, she whined, growled, woofed, and stared out the open side doors as if wanting Verna's attention. Thinking nothing amiss, Verna absently said, "Quiet, Girl. We'll be home soon. Ya gotta hold it til then." As she leaned forward to grab bundles needed at that spot, Questra sailed over her head and disappeared into the rainy dark. Verna couldn't see past the streetlight's cone of light and was so shocked at Questra's unexpected vault, she stood speechless for a moment.

Then she heard growling and snarling, and a male voice shout, "A'right, a'right...get it offa me...get it off! Ow! Ow! Dammit! Hey! Guys! Get it offa me..."

"Questra! Come!" Verna called, and the noise stopped. The beautiful German Shepherd trotted gracefully into the light where Verna stood. Her ruff erect, she kept turning back toward the dark, growling and lunging threateningly. Verna saw five figures running past a streetlight across the park. Questra looked up, woofed, and reared up, her paws on Verna's shoulders, as if confirming Verna was okay.

"Wow, Girl. I guess you showed *them* a thing or two didn't you!" Verna quickly stacked the bundles at the spot, climbed in the van, called Questra, and closed the side doors. She hugged her dog, and got behind the wheel. Questra resumed her place in the passenger seat, sitting erect, one paw on the dash. Verna completed her delivery run and drove back to the warehouse to report the incident.

"So, there I was on the Morningside run, next to the van counting papers for the park spot, bagging bundles, and my dog sails out of the van and, apparently, chased some guys across the park. I didn't even see 'em til they ran through the light of a streetlight on the opposite side." Verna was breathless with the telling.

Joseph Couch – big-bodied, soft-featured, and gentle-natured – was the current lead, as leads rotated among all the warehouses every six weeks. He was the friendliest of all the ones she'd met. He peered thoughtfully now at Verna over his steaming coffee mug. Incidents of Seattle Times employees encountering trouble during night deliveries were rare, but did happen.

"Did you see their faces, Verna?" He laid aside his crossword puzzle and gave her his full attention.

"No. I didn't see anything at all because of the brightness from the pole light overhead. Questra jumped over me and chased 'em off." She gestured over her head with one arm. Verna started to shake as the adrenaline drained away. "Good thing I had my dog with me. I don't know what they might have done, but whatever they had in mind, it didn't happen." There was an open package of powdered sugar doughnuts on Joe's desk, and he shoved it towards her in invitation. She took one and chewed. "All I could see was five guys running hell bent for election out the other side of the park. I saw 'em when they ran under the pole light." She swallowed. "What should I do? Do I have to make a report of some kind, or anything?" She sat, powdered sugar white around her mouth like a clown's make-up, shudders visibly rippling through her.

Joseph pondered a moment, with a ham-like hand reached in a desk drawer, and handed her a sheet of paper. "This is an incident report form. Go ahead an' fill it out." He slid it across to her. "I think you're done for tonight. Get this finished an' just go on home, okay?"

"Thank you," she sighed gratefully. Then thought a moment as she began filling in the blanks. "Uh...Joe...if this had happened to one of the other spotters instead of me, would you be sending them home early?" She paused, pen in mid-air.

He deliberated, debated with himself, considered his report to his supervisor. "Well...since none-a them's got a hunnerd pound dog ridin' shotgun, it might be me here fillin' out a very different report if they'd been jumped, say, an' their vehicle stolen, say." He shrugged. "However, you handled it great, an' even finished yer run. I think unner these circumstances it's okay for you ta go on home. I'll deliver yer other run myself." He reached under the desk for his enormous stainless steel thermos. A hunter and fisherman, he took his thermos with him wherever he went. He pulled a paper cup from the dispenser next to the water fountain, filled it with coffee from his thermos, and gave it to Verna. "You got Hawthorne tonight fer tha second run, right? I'll go soon as Paulie gets back, an' he can watch out fer things while I'm gone." He gestured to the paper cup. "My wife, Jean, makes my coffee, so it's super strong jus' tha way I like it. You might wanna put some-a that creamer stuff in it. I swear sometimes she adds gunpowder." He grinned, shrugged into his parka, and left, closing the office door and leaving Verna alone with her report and her special coffee. She reached for another powdered sugar doughnut, shivered, and continued filling in the report.

Christmas was upon them. Verna and Jerry grew more and more distant. The stress of her five days and two nights a week schedule, and the constant barrage of arguments relating to possibly building a new house, took their toll on the relationship. Verna's main comfort was her dog. Questra went with her everywhere. Verna took her to Doctor Griffin's clinic for her annual shots, and he mentioned a cat abandoned at the hospital.

"She's a sweet girl, really. Just a little stand offish. As a rule, cats like me, but this one, well...she more or less just tolerates me. She's a tabby point Siamese with the bluest eyes I've ever seen. I'll have to send her to the shelter. There's no answer at her owner's phone number and there's no other contact information. She's been here over a month since her spay."

Verna looked up from Questra on the exam table and asked, "What's her name?

"Tasha." The vet grinned. "I call her TashaKitty. Wanna say hello?"

And that was how it happened that Verna now had a dog *and* a cat.

"Happy New Year, Verna," said Jerry, hoisting a glass of champagne.

Geez...Nineteen Seventy Nine had <u>better</u> be a happy year...or happier than last year, at least...Nineteen Seventy Eight wasn't too happy at all!...Veronica running away...me and Jerry constantly bickering...Jerry always paranoid about money...Dear God, are You sure this is one of Your Mysterious Ways to work a wonder in my life?...oh, Heavenly Father, help my faith...and now Jerry's drinking more!

Since visiting several wineries in the area, Jerry decided drinking wine was not so terrible after all and thought to become a "wine connoisseur." Verna enjoyed visiting the wineries, but her lifetime's abstinence from alcohol did not change. Her Southern Baptist roots were deep. Anyway, she had never acquired a taste for any type of alcoholic beverage.

Verna toasted him with her stemmed glass of Ginger ale. "Here's to Nineteen Seventy Nine. May it be a good year!" *clink*

"May we move into our new house! To our new house!" Jerry responded, and drained his glass. "Ah! A perfect blend and body." He filled his glass again. "May we find a builder to build our new house this year! To our builder!" He drained and refilled his glass. "Now what shall we toast to? How about toasting the old year good riddance? Bye, bye, old year." He saluted the window with his glass, drained it again, and refilled it once more. "Ya got a toast, Verna, ol' girl?" Jerry fancied he was Humphrey Bogart in "The African Queen" at times like this. Lately he was only "relaxed and happy" after downing several drinks – actually several *bottles* – of whatever wine he was "connoisseuring" at the moment.

"How 'bout I make you a piece of toast, Jerry? Maybe it will help soak up some of that champagne." "Ah, yes! A toast to toast!" He saluted the toaster in the kitchen, drained his glass again, refilled it once more, and looked around. "Ya know…this ain't such a *bad* house. To our house here at the end of the road." Once more, drain and refill. "And a toast to the doghouse. Ya did a good job-a fixin' its leakin' roof, Verna, ol' girl. Gladja didn't move out there. Here's to it, an' here's ta you!"

Nineteen Seventy Nine was the year Jerry became an active alcoholic. It was not the year he and Verna found a builder to build their new house, however. Nor was it the next year. Or the next. Five years would pass from Jerry's 1979 New Year's toast to their new house and its builder. During those years they would put down earnest money on land to build a log house but discover it would be too distant from the city to be feasible; they would come close to buying or building others, but there would always be some hindrance obstructing them. Friction between them continued to grow during those years. And Jerry's alcoholic dysfunction increased.

There had been no word on Veronica's disappearance. It was as if she vanished. They received a birth announcement from Anne Marie and Patrick. A baby daughter. *Now Susanna will be the big sister…that will be good for her.*

Doctor Hale worked with Verna on remaining mentally and emotionally stable during her monthly visits.

"You must be as vigilant and careful of your mental health as you are your physical health. For instance, you get an annual flu shot, right? You eat well, get adequate rest, fresh air, etc., right?"

"Well, Doctor Hale, I mostly eat well, but I do drink an awful lot of coffee, and we always have doughnuts or some other kind of pastry at work, and I am partial to chocolate. I do get a flu shot every year, of course." Verna reached for the candy dish on the side table by the timer clock, today filled with silver-foil-wrapped chocolate kisses. Doctor Hale did not allow smoking in his office or waiting area, so he compensated with candy. "As to the fresh air and exercise, though, I can attest to both of those. Daily. Or nightly as the case may be."

"Ah, yes. Were your would-be assailants ever found or identified?" Doctor Hale unwrapped a kiss and popped it in his mouth.

Verna shook her head. "Trouble is, though, after that story got around, many of the other spotters brought their dogs with them on their runs. The company received complaints about dogs barking, or crapping on lawns, or just being a nuisance in general. So corporate ruled no dogs in vans, no way, no how, no excuses. My dog was trained. She stayed in the passenger seat away from my load and didn't get out of the van except that one night when she protected me." Verna shook her head in disgust. "I was raised to always keep my dog under my control." She took a deep breath and sat back in the chair.

Doctor Hale smiled slightly under his mustache. "Verna, is there any word on your daughter? Have you had any more dreams of her?" Doctor Hale was always interested to hear about his patients' dreams. Sometimes they were the subconscious communicating something.

She sighed deeply and leaned forward. "Yes, I have had several dreams, but I can't tell if they're the 'Dream Travel' kind like you've mentioned, or, if in my imagining the worst, my brain provides a visual of that imagining. Recently, I've seen a girl from the back, walking along the shoulder of a highway wearing a black backpack and accompanied by a brindle dog that is either a boxer or a pitbull. I never see her face, just the back of a denim jacket, a baseball cap with longish brown hair sticking out from under it, and a dog alongside. She has her thumb out, hitchhiking. Sometimes she wears a bandana on her head and I almost get close enough to get in front of her to see her face, but that's where I wake up. In tears." Verna looked down at her hands in her lap. "I should never have allowed my girls to go to Tucson!" Verna stood, propelled to her feet by the surge of adrenaline from the angry regret that chewed its way through her.

Doctor Hale sat calmly and waited. Verna walked to the window and looked out at the rainy expanse of parking lot. She returned to her seat. "Verna, do you believe you would somehow know if...if your daughter were...not alive?"

She nodded vehemently. "Yes. I firmly believe I would know, and in my heart I feel she is alive. And, somehow, I think she is okay. As okay as a teen-ager out in the world alone *can* be, I guess. No one knows her like I do. She's an amazing person. Back when I was pregnant and had to stay on bed rest, or, as my doctor said, "Horizontal, ja," she somehow took charge. She cooked the meals, cleaned the house, did laundry, managed her homework, and made excellent grades. Well, in everything but math, that is." Verna shrugged in embarrassment. "She inherited my inability with numbers. But my point is, if ever there was somebody born to manage on her own, it's my eldest daughter." The clock chimed, and Doctor Hale stood.

"Guard your mental health, Verna. I doubt seriously you will ever find yourself in a catatonic state again, but Depression is something that can occur in anyone at any time. You have the prescription I gave you. Don't hesitate to fill it if needed. I leave that up to you." They parted at the door. As she started out, she turned back and impulsively threw her arms about his neck for a hug. He stepped back. "Now, now, my dear. No hugging the doctor." He chuckled to soften the words. "That's not on the prescription list."

MUSIC AND MICHELLE

A poet would say music was the thread that stitched the fabric of Verna's soul coat together. Actually, since she loved to crochet, it was multi-colored variegated yarn from which her remarkable talent crocheted a melodious cloak of many colors to swaddle her musical spirit as she once swaddled newborns in Orlando's Memorial Hospital. Born into a "singing family," music was imprinted upon her young psyche in early childhood as she fell asleep on the sun-soaked boards of her front porch while neighbors gathered with her "grownups" to "sing the sun down" in an Oklahoma twilight. Verna's formative years were marinated in a milieu of music as her father constantly sang at home, as did his mother, Verna's Grandmother Davidson, who lived with them. Her family sang together in their car whenever they drove anywhere. Verna sang through her young days as she groomed her horses, picked peas from the family's garden, or sat in a patio chair with her dog lying at her feet. Throughout high school she sang as an award-winning soloist in Lawton's high school's statewide acclaimed, blue-ribbon choir. She sang as an adult to her infant daughters in Tucson, while endlessly ironing in her Orlando drab duplex, and as she hauled Seattle Times newspaper bundles through drippy, rainy days with her German Shepherd, Questra, sitting in the van's passenger seat and howling with her song.

Music reached through the thick pudding of Verna's catatonia when Music Therapists Tom Nation and David Leonard quietly sang "Amazing Grace" in Tucson's Mesquite Valley Mental Hospital and she began to sing also. When Tom gently placed his guitar in Verna's hands, fitted her fingers around a chord, and she strummed her first strum, the tonal vibrations from the guitar against her chest quivered deep into her being, shivering into her very blood. Music helped return her to wholeness as Tom taught her guitar chords, and she taught songs in Music Therapy sessions – songs she sang in long ago church camps and led as Devotions Leader in her Nursing School class.

Sherry Carter, a fellow OR Nurse at Tucson's St. Joseph's hospital, allowed Verna to borrow her guitar and play it while she was in Mesquite Valley. Verna's psychological team utilized the guitar and music as poignant techniques in her psyche's healing. Upon her release from Mesquite Valley, Verna resumed rooming with Sherry and continued playing her friend's guitar. She played it often. A guitar became significant in Verna's life, almost essential to her well-being, nearly as elemental to her spirit as her deeply-rooted singing. After she married Jerry, she had no guitar, and, save for the "misty rainbow drive into Seattle," she only sang alone.

Verna's routes of newspaper bundle-hauling were done for the day. As she drove home, she noticed a music store with guitars displayed in its front wndow. There happened to be an empty parking space directly in front of the store. *An empty space right in front of the store! A "sign," maybe?...Hmmm...I'll drive around the block, and if that parking space is still empty, I'll pull in and go into the store...I mean, it couldn't hurt to just look at guitars...I'll just drive around the block and see if that space is still empty when I come back around...then I'll go in."*

She drove. It was. She did.

"How kin I he'p ya t'day?" asked the cheerful clerk. His nametag read "Carl."He wore a Hard Rock Café tee shirt, jeans, Keds, and a wide, toothy grin.

"Afternoon. Uh...well, I'd like to look at your guitars." Verna's gaze swept past the young man as she surveyed a display of guitars hanging on the wall. As she continued sweeping the store with astonished eyes, she realized there were also guitars in stands on the floor. *Wow!...this is guitar heaven...they're everywhere!*

"Sure thing. Uh...you in-ter-es-ted in acoustic...electric?..."

"Oh, acoustic. Definitely acoustic."

A pale blonde wood guitar with black headstock and dark brown pick guard caught her wandering scrutiny as if an angelic spotlight suddenly shone upon it, dimming all other instruments into guitar grayness. It was the most beautiful thing she'd ever seen. Its smooth simplicity eclipsed all others. She pointed. "I'd like to see that one."

Carl held it gently, almost reverently, and handed it to Verna. She smiled at the feel of it. "Thank you, Carl." She held it a moment, then looked at him. "Do you play?"

"Heck, yeah! I started workin' here back when I'se in high school, an' been workin' here ever since." He grinned widely; his blue eyes danced. He gestured to a stool. "Have a seat. Try 'er out. She's got a sweet tone, an' I think you'll find yer fingers can wrap around 'er pretty easy. Got a narrow neck, see? An' real smooth fret action cuz tha strings lay so close to tha board."

Verna sat, cradled the beautiful instrument, carefully fitted her fingers to a G chord, strummed, and felt the instrument's rich vibration through her chest and right into her heart, much the same as that first strum on Tom Nation's guitar. This was the sweetest sound she'd ever heard. Until this very moment she hadn't realized just how much she'd missed a guitar. She played "Amazing Grace" as she hummed along.

"Ya play gospel music, do ya?" Carl, Verna noticed, had very large ears that protruded from his head like radar dishes. He sat opposite her, his face soft with a gentle smile.

"I'm just learning. I only played a little when I lived in Tucson. Then we moved here to Seattle, and, well, I've been sorta busy ever since." To her surprise,

Verna felt tears rising and quelled them quickly. "Amazing Grace was the first song I learned."

"We offer lessons here if yer in-ter-es-ted. Buddy gives 'em. He owns tha store, see, an' he loves ta he'p people." The entrance door bell jingled, and Carl rose. "You g'wan an' keep playin'. Sounds sweet."

Verna sat for an hour and played through the songs she'd learned. Soon, though, her tender fingers began to hurt. She chuckled to herself.

Well…my hands are callused from the newspaper bundles, but the calluses I had from playing Sherry's guitar are gone…if I'm ever gonna play a guitar again, I gotta get those calluses back…

Carl reappeared. "Well, whaddaya think? Ain't 'at a sweet sound? I tol' ya she had a sweet sound."

"How much is it?"

"On tha neck there, right onna tag is tha price. Lemme see…" He reached for the small white tag. "Twelve hunnerd dollars. Yep." He stood back.

"Wow! I didn't realize guitars were so costly." Even as she spoke the words, Verna's hands tightened their hold of their own accord. She gulped. "Do you have anything…uh…cheaper?" Hastily, she added, "This nice. This…sweet. But maybe a little less money?"

Carl frowned in thought. "Wellll…yeah. We do have sump'n cheap, butcha won't git 'at smooth sweet sound from a cheap guitar." He peered around the store as if trying to remember which ones might be cheaper and still have a nice sound.

In a blink, Verna decided. This was *her* guitar! "Never mind. I want this one." She smiled at him. "This one. For sure." She followed him to the cash register. "Do you have a case for it?"

When Verna left the store, she had written a check for the guitar, a strap, a case, a pack of picks, and a songbook for beginners. Fortunately, Tom Nation had sketched chords for her, so she understood chord diagrams.

Jerry was late getting home that evening. He was "working late" more and more these days. Verna kept dinner warm in the oven. She sat on the couch with the songbook open on the coffee table. Tasha was stretched full length on top of the back of the couch where warm air from the baseboard heaters made it cozy. When the front door opened, Verna smelled Jerry before she saw him. And what she smelled wasn't wine.

"Jerry? What in the world?" She stood apart from him in the living room as he removed his coat. He swayed slightly and looked at her from under his cap bill like a frog peering from under a lily pad. His eyes were glassy.

"Colonel Dickershon…uh…Dickerson…pashed…uh…passed…aw…passed away. T'day. We toassed…uh…toasted 'im." He looked at Verna with an air of defiance. "See…itch whatchu…uh…whatchu do inna Air Nashnul Guard." He lifted his hands helplessly, as if the decision had not been his. One hand on the wall for balance, he turned and walked toward the bedroom to hang up his coat.

He's been drinking hard liquor!

Verna was suddenly wary. Wine she maybe could understand, living in wine country as they did, but hard liquor was something else entirely. *Oh, God!…not another alcoholic again!*

"Well, I'm sorry to hear about Colonel Dickerson. Do you know when the funeral will be?"

"Dunno," said Jerry from the depths of his closet. "Prolly gonna be inna 'is hometown, though…not here." He reappeared attired in jeans and turtleneck. "Wha's that?" He indicated the black guitar case laying on the couch, songbook open on the coffee table.

"My new guitar. I've really missed playing, and I stopped today on the way home and bought one. Wanna hear?" She smiled.

Jerry stood, swaying ever so slightly, as if keeping his balance on a ship at sea, frowning at the guitar. With effort, he lifted his head and looked at her. "You bough…uh…bought a guitar?" He frowned. "Why?"

"Because I…well…I was just beginning to get the hang of it when we left Tucson, and I miss it. You play piano, and I…" Her voice trailed off as she gestured at the guitar.

Jerry advanced toward the guitar case. Verna hastily moved to open it, picked up the guitar, placed the strap around her neck, and strummed a G chord. "See? Isn't that a sweet sound? The clerk explained all about the wood this guitar is made of and why it has such a mellow, lovely tone. Listen." She played "Amazing Grace," strumming only with her fingers, no pick. Jerry stood, looking disdainfully at it.

"How mush did it cos'?"

"Well, the guitar was twelve hundred dollars, but I also bought a case, a strap, a songbook, and some picks." She grinned, happy with her prize.

Jerry stood agape, speechless. Then, his slurring gone…"You'll take it back! You'll take that right back to tha store an' get tha money back! We can't afford for you ta go buyin' things like a…a…twelve hundred dollar guitar!" He roared. "Take it back!"

Verna's jaw dropped, and she quickly replaced the guitar in the case and latched it closed for its protection.

Suddenly it feels like I'm back with Patrick again…what's next?…oh, Dear God in Heaven…

Jerry yanked the case roughly off the couch by the handle, and the weight of it caused him to lose his balance. He fell heavily on the coffee table. Verna, anxious that the guitar not get damaged, took it out of his hand and hugged it with both arms in front of her.

He managed to raise himself off the coffee table and stood, swaying slightly, scowling. Verna took a step back, frightened, tightly holding the guitar in its case. He raised his finger and pointed at her.

"You. Will. Take. It. Back!" His face was dark with rage, suffused with blood. Verna wondered what his blood pressure must be at the moment.

Questra stood in the living room doorway, ruff raised, lips lifted in a quiet snarl, a low growl deep in her chest. Verna, having trained her with hand signals, signaled "Down. Stay." Reluctantly, Questra dropped on her belly in the doorway, but she kept up the low growl.

"In the van. Right now!" Jerry commanded in a rough, threatening voice.

Verna decided discretion was the better part of valor and grabbed her purse and keys. She gestured to Questra to lie down under the piano. "Stay, Girl," she muttered.

Verna got in the driver's side of the van, setting the guitar down carefully behind the driver's seat. Jerry appeared at her window.

"I'll drive," he croaked, and yanked on the door handle. Verna automatically always locked the door when she got in the van, and she had done so. She lowered the window a bit and said, "No, Jerry, I'll drive. You don't know where it is." She looked at him." And I'm afraid you're drunk."

With a snarl, Jerry got in the passenger side. Neither of them wore a coat.

"You want to what?" Verna thought the man behind the counter must be the owner, Buddy, whom Carl mentioned when she was in the store earlier. He wore no nametag.

"My wife said she wants to return this guitar she bought here earlier today." Jerry's voice was now low and controlled, and he wasn't weaving as much. He reeked of liquor.

"Why? Is something the matter with it?" The man looked from Jerry to Verna in costernation.

"Sir, there is nothing wrong with this guitar. My husband, here, just thinks it's something beyond the budget." Verna laid the case on the glass counter, unlatched it, and the guitar shone in its honey-blonde wood splendor. The very sight of it stirred Verna's heart.

Carefully, the man lifted the guitar out of the case. "Do you have your receipt?"

"Yes, it's right here." Verna laid the slip of paper on the glass counter.

"You bought this guitar from Carl today? Did you play it first? Try it out?" He fished his glasses from a shirt pocket.

"Yes. A little. I played through what songs I know. I'm still learning." Verna smiled.

Glasses in place, the man glanced at the receipt, and his eyebrows shot up. "Carl sold you *this* guitar for twelve hundred dollars?"

"Yes. See? The tag is still on the neck there." Verna indicated the small white tag that clearly indicated $1,200.00.

Jerry observed this exchange in bleary exasperation. "Look, buddy, don't give us any hassle. Just refund my wife's money. Or just tear up the check. Take it back." He placed both hands on the countertop and leaned heavily forward, threatening.

Addressing Verna, the man said, "Ma'am, Carl made an error. This is the wrong tag." He gestured to another guitar hanging in a rack on the wall. *"That* guitar is twelve hundred dollars. *This* guitar," he touched it gently, lovingly, "sells for *twenty five* hundred dollars."

Verna gasped, the sudden air intake making her a bit dizzy. "Really?"

"Say again," said Jerry. He had straightened up now and appeared to be returning somewhat to normal. More or less.

"I said, *this* guitar sells for twenty five hundred dollars. But, since you've already bought it, and obviously you have since you have a receipt, it's yours for the amount you've already paid." He shrugged and gently laid the guitar back in its plush case.

Verna looked at Jerry and squinted. "Music therapy," she said.

He took a step back from the counter, hands up in defeat. "Music therapy."

Back in the van, guitar once again behind the driver's seat, Verna said, "Jerry, I need you to hear me. Are you yourself yet?" She used her nurse's training to command her voice to be calm and rational.

He nodded, then said, "Uh-huh."

"You may not speak to me that way. Ever again. It is our financial agreement that I have a spending account, you have a spending account, and we have a joint account from which we buy things for the house and meet household expenses. I bought this guitar from my own spending account." She signaled the turn into their street, headlights shining down the wet pavement. "I do not answer to you about money that is designated as my own." She pulled into their driveway, put the van in park, and turned off the ignition. "Are we clear? I am not your ex, Mary Ann, who intentionally sabotaged the credit card accounts. I am your wife. Your partner in the entire enterprise called marriage." She looked at him in the gloom, his face a pale splotch. "Apparently, I got a very good deal on a very good guitar. But if he had said I needed to pay the rest of the price in order to have it, I would have paid it."

Reluctantly, Jerry nodded and opened his door, the gloom dispelled by the dome light.

Back inside the house, Questra sniffed Verna as if to assure herself her human was okay. She sniffed the guitar case, and even sniffed Verna's purse. But the beautiful dog merely looked at Jerry and did not approach him. Verna patted her shoulders and invited Questra to come up to her where she could scratch her behind the ears. Questra reared up, rested her paws on Verna's shoulders, licked Verna's chin, and happily wagged her tail, glad the threat to her world was over.

Tasha meowed a greeting from the back of the couch, as she was apparently interested in dinner.

The dinner in the oven was ruined. They sat at the table with cheese and crackers. Jerry had not spoken since the van. He rose and opened a bottle of wine. Verna sat, quite still, observing her "non-drinking" husband who had developed quite a taste for all things alcoholic.

Next he'll be drinking beer and watching football…drunk on weekends…just like Patrick.

Verna rose, got a wine glass, took the Ginger ale out of the refrigerator, and sat down once more.

"By the way, Jerry, I've named my guitar 'Michelle.' Shall we drink a toast to her?"

"Uh…er…um…well, a twenty five hundred dollar guitar for only twelve hundred dollars?…that's less than half the price…uh, sure…good bargain…yeah, good bargain…to, uh…to Michelle."

Clink.

Verna heard a song inside her head. In that gray gap that is not quite sleep nor wakefulness – that murkiness of mind between both worlds where inspiration may be found – she distinctly heard herself singing as she strummed her guitar. She felt the heaviness of the guitar, her fingers fretting chords, the solid roundness of the strings. As she came completely awake, the song followed her out of sleep. She arose, reached for Michelle, placed her fingers in chord position, strummed, and sang the song. Startled, she looked at her fingers as if she'd not seen them before. The song began again, so she played it once more as she accompanied herself singing it. Scrabbling for paper and pen, she wrote the words and placed correct chords above them. What had clearly, but vaporously, circled around and around inside her brain was now solidly embodied in ink on paper. Now she could actually see it with her eyes, hear it with her mind, play it with her fingers, and sing it with her voice. It was real! She couldn't have been more astonished than if she had just laid an egg.

Huh!…how 'bout that!…I wrote a song!….me…a real, honest-to-goddness song!…words and all…chords…a whole, entire, complete song!

The song, born of a dream about her daughter, was sad; yet it was a great comfort. She entitled the song "Little Girl Gone" since it was about Veronica, her little girl runaway, her little girl gone. As she sang, she thought about Susanna and what song she would write about her youngest. She sighed, hoping she would dream about Susanna; perhaps a song would arise from sleep as Veronica's had. She wondered what song she would write for Chrissy.

Verna continued to practice on Michelle and write songs, though sporadically due to her work constraints as well as Jerry's belittling behaviors and disdainful attitudes toward her music. Jerry played at playing the piano and fancied himself somewhat of a musician, although he really only constantly played scales – up and down the keyboard, up and down for hours as he conceived himself an accomplished pianist practicing his art. His derisive attitude toward Verna's music was born out of ridiculous jealousy, laughable had it not arisen from such a serious emotional disorder. He seemed to have forgotten the miracle of music he witnessed in Mesquite Valley Mental Hospital when music reached into Verna's darkness, flicked on a light, and led her out of catatonia. Jerry did not appreciate Verna's talent, was intimidated by it, and she realized that. She rarely played Michelle or sang one of her songs in front of him because he never grasped or respected what she did.

Verna practiced and sang in secret. As she did, she was fond of remembering Jesus' words as recorded in Matthew. "When thou prayest, enter into thy closet, and when thou hast shut thy door, pray to thy Father which is in secret; and thy Father which seeth in secret shall reward thee openly." So she "entered into her closet," practiced, and sang in secret. It became a compulsion for her, playing Michelle until her fingers blistered and her mind drained of lyrics, and she knew not why she was so compelled. Yet, in secret, she unkowingly prepared for the accolades with which her Father would one day openly reward her. That day was yet to come as if coming from a Scriptural "far country" far, far away. But it was coming, and, somewhere deep in her depths, Verna's spirit knew and compelled her to continue her efforts.

ERUPTIONS, ASHES, AND A
GREEN DOT.

The year was 1980. As spring exploded in a hot pink blaze of rhododendrons and azaleas, the entire Seattle area experienced small tremors and minor earthquake shocks. A Washington State volcano, Mount St. Helens, was stirring, and, according to all reports, was preparing to erupt. Verna paid no attention to such reports. Her mind was occupied with work, paying bills, Jerry's deterioration, attending church, staying sane, writing songs, and notating her dreams. Doctor Hale suggested she keep a dream journal.

She was convinced that, somehow, her subconscious had the ability to go to her daughters, wherever they were, in her "dreamself state." Her dreams were vivid, lucid, *real,* and involved all her senses except touch. In one, she saw Susanna's hair had grown long as she was present during an argument with Anne Marie, Susanna insisting indignantly, with a firm stomp of a small foot, she would rather die than cut her hair short ever again. In her dream, Verna inhaled the herbal fragrance of Susanna's hair but could not touch it. She ached to be able to run her fingers through her daughter's hair once more.

In another dream she saw Susanna holding her baby sister whose tiny fist was entwined in that long hair. Susanna yelled for somebody to make the baby let go. Verna's dreamself blew into the baby's face, causing her to be surprised and open her hands. Verna could not prove that such events actually happened, but she felt in her heart they did.

She dreamt of seeing someone she felt certain was Veronica – long, straight, light brown hair, head wrapped in a blue bandana, faded denim jacket and jeans, denim backpack embroidered with flowers and symbols. The person walked along cheerfully, accompanied by two dogs, the familiar brindled, smooth-coated dog and a bigger brown-and-white fluffier one. Saint Bernard, perhaps? With a hiss of airbrakes, an 18-wheeler stopped, and the girl ran to get in, dogs loping happily behind. Verna's dreamself called out, "Veronica! No! Don't ride with strangers!" The enormous rig pulled away with a belch of black diesel smoke, and Verna jolted awake, crying, calling out as she had in her dream. She immediately recorded the dream in her journal.

Sunday, May 18, 1980. Verna was home alone. It was a rare Sunday off for her. Jerry was with his Air National Guard unit, as they had been called to duty because of the menace of the mountain. A tremor rippled under the house, rattling dishes in their cupboards and rolling the floor like small waves. She turned on the television. It was 8:40am, and it was headline news! At 8:32am Mount St. Helens burst open! Its entire north face collapsed, releasing superheated gases and magma in a massive lateral blast. A glowing cloud of gas and rocks was blown out of the mountain's face, moving at nearly supersonic speed, instantaneously obliterating everything within eight miles. The shockwave blew through surrounding forest for nineteen miles, leveling century-old trees, all trunks lying neatly aligned pointing north as if a Cosmic Giant had laid them out in a game of pick-up sticks. Nearby Spirit Lake boiled like a cauldron, and then its water was completely displaced by a followng avalanche.

Shortly after the initial lateral explosion, a vertical eruption occurred at the mountain's summit, sending a mushroom cloud of ash and gases more than twelve miles into the air. Over the next few days, an estimated five hundred and forty million tons of ash settled over seven states. As soon as it was humanly possible, crews of First Responders, Jerry's unit among them, were sent to the area to "work the mountain."

The next day, Monday, at 11:00am, Seattle Times Circulation Supervisor Gary Lawson assembled the entire Lake City Distribution Warehouse crew. He announced that, no matter the nature of a national emergency, the paper always went out, volcanic ash or no volcanic ash. Many questioned the decision, especially of driving vehicles in ash that could destroy engines as well as human lungs. Gary pronounced Management would address malfunctioning vehicles; employees should wear surgical masks donated by area hospitals and take other protective precautions. But the paper would go out! He retreated to his office, removing his whiskey flask from his hip pocket as he walked. Verna, van loaded with much sought-after news, cranked up her Johnny Cash tape and set out. It seemed that she had already absorbed so many shocks in her life, somehow a volcanic eruption and possibility that ash might permanently damage her engine or lungs barely registered. She did as always. Her father's daughter, she soldiered on.

Verna's dreamself skimmed lightly over a forest floor. There were pine needles, pine cones, vines, and rocks under her. It was dark because the forest was so dense. She smelled the turpentine scent of pine, the freshness of air so clean it purified everything it touched. She heard the deep "woof" of a big dog and turned her attention in that direction. On the one hand, she knew she was sleeping in her bed, but, on the other, she knew she was traveling, her single purpose to find her daughter. The "woof" came again. She was getting closer. There. A flash of blue. A blue bandanna wrapped around shining light brown hair. Verna's dreamself descended. There she was. Veronica running through the forest, a smell of fear clinging to her. There was just one dog with her, the big brown and white one, bounding along ahead, leading her through the trees. Verna's dreamself wafted up and saw a cliff in the near distance – an abrupt sharp edge to a drop of several hundred feet. Veronica didn't know it was there, and, if she kept running, she would run right off the cliff edge and fall to her death.

Verna shouted at her, trying to warn her of the imminent danger. But no sound came. The dog now ran back and forth along the cliff's edge, barking. She heard Veronica say, "Hush, Kitty! Shut up!" The dog stopped frantically running and pricked up its ears. Verna saw the fine hairs on its face. Definitely St. Bernard genes. Its paws resting on the rocky outcrop were huge. Verna lowered her dreamself, still shouting at Veronica to stop. Finally she came alongside her and blew. It caused Veronica to stumble; her backpack strap caught on a branch, bringing her to an abrupt halt. Flailing frantically behind her trying to reach it, Veronica was pinned to the spot.

Now Verna heard the pursuers – two men. One had something dark in his hand and was hollering. "Stop! Hey you! Kid! I said stop!" He was dressed in a red plaid shirt, black denim jeans, and worn boots." The other man wore a blue chambray shirt and denim jacket. There was something shiny in his hand, metal glinting in the twilight. He was running so hard he had no breath to yell with. Verna saw his face was dark with anger and exertion. The other man spoke. "Do you see her anywhere? Where in the hell is she?"

"Dunno, Jake. I did hear 'at damn dogga hers, though. She gotta be close!"

Verna's dreamself saw Veronica struggling with the back strap entangled on the branch. She spoke to her dog in a harsh whisper. "Kitty! Here girl." The big dog bounded up, tongue lolling as if enjoying a fun game. "Lay down! Shush!" The dog dropped heavily to her stomach and closed her mouth. The two men ran past, heavy boots thudding through the stillness of the forest. Somewhere above a hawk screeched. Verna's dreamself stayed with Veronica. She saw her face plainly now, sweating with exertion. In the distance two high, thin screams diminished into silence. The pursuers had reached the cliff's edge and fell into hundreds of feet of nothingness. Veronica's expression was one of incredulity. Just then the branch snapped, and she tumbled to the ground. The big dog raised its head and woofed once more.

"Verna! Verna! Get up. Come out here! I need you to help me!" It was Jerry's voice in the forest, coming from far away somewhere in the trees. But Jerry was with his squad "working the mountain" with radar communication trucks, assisting on search and rescue. *Jerry, did you fall over the cliff, too?*

"C'mon, Verna, get up and come out here!"

Groggily, Verna fought herself awake, not wanting to leave Veronica in her dream, and realized there was a cold draft in the house. She got up to investigate and saw a green glowing dot in her dark living room. She heard another soft "woof." *Why is that dream dog still barking?...and a lightning bug in my living room?...how did a lightning bug get in my house?...but there aren't any fireflies in Seattle...and how did it open the door?...* It took Verna a few moments to realize the cold draft was from the open living room door, the glowing green dot was a glow-stick in Jerry's uniform pocket, and the "woofs" were from Questra as she announced Jerry's arrival.

"Come on outside an' help me. I gotta get outta this. I gotta get a shower." The green light from the glow-stick reflected eerily off the grayness of his face, and Verna realized he was covered in ash. She followed him outside.

"Help me get this uniform off. I wanna get as little of this ash in tha house as possible. Come on."

Verna, clad only in her robe, followed him out the front door. He stood in the driveway, an ash-shrouded, gray scarecrow, arms outstretched as if on a cross in a cornfield, wisps of ash wafting off him with every slight movement. "Buttons! Undo tha damn buttons!"

Dutifully, Verna reached for the buttons on his jacket and realized Jerry wore gloves. Every touch sent a cascade of fine talc-like ash falling to the ground. As smoothly as possible, she worked the jacket off his arms and dropped it. Next the shirt, as gently as possible. Jerry stepped away from the fallen jacket, and every step caused a fountain of fine ash to puff up from his boots. She peeled his shirt off and unbuckled his belt. Then she knelt down to his boots. She unlaced them through the crusty, clinging ash and helped him remove them. Not an easy task to do while standing. Boots off, he was able to peel down his pants, and was finally free of the ash-laden uniform.

"Now my hair. Can you get this nasty stuff outta my hair?"

Verna raked her fingers through her husband's hair as swirls of ash showered down. He shook his head to release more, fine ash flying like sand from a shaking bison rising from a sand roll.

"There ya go. Gee, I had no idea this stuff was like this," Verna said in wonder. "Let's get you into the shower now."

Leaving the filthy clothes where they lay, she led Jerry into the house. Finally turning on a light, she saw him for the first time. His hair and face were ashen gray, streaked with runnels of perspiration. He leaned over the sink, scooped handfuls of water, and splashed them over his face and into his mouth, rinsing and spitting.

"Oh, God, that's better," he said, finally straightening up. "Now for a shower. Wouldja get me a clean uniform ready? I'm here ta get some supplies from tha office, an' I'm doin' all this on Guard time." He peeled off his tee shirt and briefs, stepped into the shower, and pulled the curtain closed.

Verna laid out fresh uniform pants and shirt. Then she went to see about the jacket. He only had one, which he needed, so she laid it over a webbed chair in the yard and smacked it with her hand to beat some ash out of it. She was in rather a surrealistic state, having awakened out of "Dream Travel" to a green dot in her darkened, cold living room. Awakening so abruptly to Jerry's unorthodox entry, it felt somehow as if part of her was still "out there" wherever Veronica was. Smacking the jacket and raising clouds of gray ash was bringing her into the "here and now" in a very real way.

Jerry emerged from the front door, carrying his lunchbox and thermos. He reached for the ashy jacket and put it on. Then he bent to kiss her. "Thanks, Sweetheart. I gotta get back to the mountain. Thanks for helping me. You can go back to sleep now." He got in his ash-covered jeep and sped away, gray ash billowing behind it as if it were a flock of ostriches stampeding on Sahara sand dunes.

Verna went in the house and made coffee. As she sipped, she reflected on her dream. *Was that real? Was Veronica really in danger? Did I actually intervene somehow, some way? Could I really have been there in spirit and blew upon her?* Years ago, she remembered, in Orlando's Oak Creek Methodist Church, one of Reverend James' sermons was on "the breath of the spirit." He explained the Hebrew word relating to spirit is *"rauch,"* meaning "air in motion," or "breath." It also means "life." Linking "breath" with "air in motion," it means "spirit." Reverend James described how the "Breath of Life" was blown by God into Creation as He spoke His Word, and within His Word was His Breath. Reverend James said we all have that "Breath of God," the "Breath of Holy Spirit," within us for we literally breathe "the Breath of God" first breathed when Time began. *Wow! What a concept! How marvelous are the works of the Lord!*

Perhaps that was what happened when her dreamself blew, like when she blew into the baby's face to surprise her and make her let go of Susanna's hair. Perhaps that was what happened tonight. She blew the breath of the spirit and caused her daughter to stumble, which caused the strap to catch on the branch, which kept her from going over the edge of the cliff as her pursuers had. Could that have happened, as implausible as it seems? *As Hamlet said to Horatio,* thought Verna, *there are more things in heaven and earth than are dreamt of in your philosophy. Yep…there sure are!*

Verna didn't go back to bed. She sat in the living room and played her song again, singing "Little Girl Gone" as a balm to soothe her spirit and settle her nerves.

TIME

T ime became a curiously malleable thing for Verna, her life segmented not so much by the printed calendar as by events printed upon her heart. Birthing Chrissy and giving her up for adoption made that birthday a milestone. Every December nineteenth she sent a birthday card to Orlando's Children's Home Society to be placed in the baby's file. Thus she soothed that part of her broken heart, believing one day the child would see them and know she was never forgotten by the woman who birthed her.

May brought memories of her graduation from Orange County Nursing School and her LPN certificate. That triumph was tempered by the sorrow of losing her daughters to her ex-husband's devious adoption scheme. Every New Year's Eve now carried with it the bizarre memory of waking up in a mental hospital, not knowing how she'd gotten there, only to learn she'd been catatonic for weeks.

In Seattle, she was in the "Era of Marriage to Jerry." She'd worked at Aurora Veterinary Clinic, and now, for years, as a spotter and trainer for The Seattle Times. The first woman driver/distributor for The Times, she fought for and won a separate women's bathroom at the warehouse, wrote a breakroom cleaning schedule, and instituted a successful annual holiday potluck, all hitherto unheard of in this blue-collar man's world.

So far, through all of "The Seattle Experience," she lived with Jerry in the small house nestled in the rhododendrons and azaleas with a plum tree growing by the front door – the little house at the end of the road. Jerry's two sons came to visit every summer, making the house much more crowded, noisy, messy, and impossible for Verna to sleep during the day. Their visits were for only two weeks, so she managed, but she came to dread those times. Her psychiatrist, Doctor Hale, continued to see her once a month. After dreaming of her oldest daughter running from danger, she resumed antidepressant medication. Via her friend, Janice in Tucson, Verna and Susanna continually exchanged letters.

1984 arrived in flurries of work, snow, ice, hazardous driving conditions, and Jerry's increased drinking. When they first met, neither of them drank alcohol. Now Jerry regularly consumed all types of alcoholic beverages; he was constantly in some state of inebriation. Verna, in her nursing years, met patients who required a small amount of alcohol each day to keep from getting Delirium Tremens, "the DTs." Sometimes DTs resulted in grand mal seizures, and Verna feared Jerry was headed for them. Liver damage was a given at his rate of consumption. He drank as if he wanted to make up for all the years he abstained when his church forbade alcohol.

"Jerry! Jerry, please turn the tv down!" Verna shambled into the den where Jerry watched a football game. She had worked the night before and had just gone to sleep when the noise woke her.

"Hey, Verna! Come siddown. We're winnin', see?" Jerry leapt to his feet and cheered a touchdown, spilling his beer. The braided rug in the den, so attractive years ago, was now blotched and stained with multiple spills from Jerry and his sons.

"Jerry, please listen to me. I worked last night. I've only been home a couple of hours, and I desperately need to sleep. I'm asking you, please turn the tv down, and please stop yelling." She turned to go back to the bedroom, the sash on her robe dragging the floor.

"No, no, no, no…it's you who's gotta come here, see? Not go back to bed. Bed's boring. Football's where it's at. I'll pour you a drink." Jerry gestured to the shelves over the bar that once featured an empty beer can collection when they bought the house. They were now stocked with every manner of spirits imaginable. A new, small fridge under the bar was stocked with beer and ale. "What'll you have? You just name it, and I'll pour it." He stood, sloppy grin on his bewhiskered face, one hand on the bar for balance.

"Jerry!" Verna yelled his name, causing a startled "woof" from Questra in the living room. Tasha retreated behind a sofa cushion, just her whiskers showing. "I worked all night! I'm dead tired. I have to go to work again tonight. I need to sleep!" She glared at him. "And you have had enough to drink for one day. Call a halt. Sober up." She turned and started for the kitchen. "I'll make you some coffee." She flinched as one of his workboots smacked the wall next to her head.

"Hey! The game's not even over. I got plenty of beer…plenty of booze…I don't want no damned coffee!" Jerry stood in the kitchen doorway, swaying slightly.

Verna picked up the boot and placed it in his hands as she walked past him. "You dropped your boot." She went into the bedroom, dressed, and emerged in warm, flannel-lined jeans, a turtleneck, a fleece sweatshirt, wool socks, and Gore-Tex boots.

"Where ya goin', Verna?"

"To where I can get some sleep. Come, Questra." She and the dog went out the living room door. The van's captain seats reclined, and she stretched out in the driver's one. Questra curled her big body in the passenger seat as best she could. Unbelievably, they both dozed. Then there was a pounding on Verna's door.

"We won! We won! Come on back inna house, Verna, ol' girl. You don' gotta shleep…sleep out here inna van for Chrissake. C'mon!" Jerry yanked on the door handle, locked as always. "Open this door, Verna! You open this door right now!" Questra stood and barked, telling him in dog language to go away and leave her pack alone.

Verna, in the middle of Jerry's yelling and Questra's barking, raised both hands in surrender. "Okay, okay, okay! All I want is some sleep, all right? Just keep the noise down so I can sleep. And for heaven's sake, stop drinking!"

She opened the door to go inside, Questra at her heel. Inside the cozy, warm house, she sat in one of the chairs at the kitchen table, sleep impossible. As she sat, she surveyed what had once seemed a pleasant place, cottage-like in its simplicity. Now it reeked of alcohol, filthy socks, sweaty clothes, and was a mess from front to back. Jerry had not put the garbage bin out for pickup on Thursday, so there were bags of beer cans and bottles against the wall in the kitchen. His dirty laundry was strewn over the couch and easy chair. Glasses and bottles sat in sticky rings on the coffee table. Helplessly, she gestured at the house. "Jerry, look. We can't live like this. Just look at this mess. I clean it up when I get home, and now, Saturday afternoon, just look at it. Look at it!" she yelled, near tears with frustration.

Jerry's face went dark with anger. "You don't tell me what to do! I follow orders alla time at work. Here in my own home, I do as I please. I drink as I please. And I watch tv just as loud as I please! Y'hear? You. Don't. Tell. Me. What. To. Do!"

This time when Verna went to the van, she started the engine and drove away, Questra in the passenger seat.

Jerry didn't drink as much when his boys were with them. He kept a pocket filled with breath mints, Verna noted, as she was the one who emptied his pockets for the laundry. He didn't seem to lose control as often when they were there.

"Hey, Brock. Hey, Jimmy. We're having barbecued pork chops tonight. Please go set the table."

Verna's request was met with grumbles and long faces, but she decided that was just par for the course for children their ages and didn't take it personally.

"Quit pushing me!" said Jimmy.

"I didn't push you hard," replied Brock. "Just a little push, like this, to get you started is all."

Brock pushed Jimmy into the wall, causing glasses on their shelves to rattle.

"Enough!" said Verna. "Boys, please just do as I asked." Eventually, order restored, dinner eaten, it was tv time. The boys argued over the channels, fighting for the remote. Jerry sat, still as a boulder in a stream, reading the newspaper, ignoring the noise.

"Boys! Stop it, Stop it right now! Give *me* the remote."

Brock threw it, causing the back to come off and the batteries to fall out as it whizzed past Verna and hit the wall. Both boys scrambled to pick it up.

"That's it!" yelled Verna. "To bed! Both of you! Right now!"

Jerry looked up. "You can't send them to bed yet. It's not bedtime." He looked at her with challenge. The boys stood uncertainly, one holding the remote, the other holding the batteries. The remote's back cover lay on the floor like a shell shed by a large insect, hollow and dead – a fitting metaphor for Verna and Jerry's marriage.

"Then you must step in and take control of them. Jerry, look around you. Look at them. This is not normal behavior." Verna was breathless and exhausted.

Jerry put down the paper. "Okay, boys. Let's go get ice cream. Get away from the mad witch of the west here, okay?" He got his keys and wallet and started for the door. Under his breath he said with menace, "You don't tell *my* boys what to do or how to behave." He scowled and walked past Verna to the front door. As the boys got their jackets and started for the door, Brock gave her the finger, and Jimmy stuck out his tongue.

In 1985 Jerry and Verna finally settled on a builder and arranged to build a new house. Progress was erratic and slow as it was difficult to coordinate both of them meeting with the builder due to Verna's schedule. Consequently, Jerry made most of the decisions, and he financially "cut corners" everywhere – no underpadding for carpets, no baseboards, used appliances instead of new ones, cheap tan kitchen linoleum instead of floor tiles, cheap light fixtures, bare minimum insulation, just cheap construction overall, a "Jerry-built house." It was hardly the wonderful, pristine new house Verna envisioned.

Once construction was finally finished, they moved into the house in March of 1986. Verna hoped having a larger living space would somewhat – *somehow* – smooth out their relationship. It didn't.

One morning Verna arose to go to work and fed Questra as usual. Questra ate with great appetite and appeared her happy, healthy doggy self. As Verna left, her dog stood on hind legs at the front fence gate, her front paws holding onto it, wagging her tail, and woofing "Good bye." Normally when Verna returned home after work, Questra waited at the gate in the same position, wagging and woofing "Hello!" This day she was not. That was not right. Something was wrong. Seriously wrong.

"Questra? Here, Girl. Where are you? Come out, come out wherever you are." Verna searched the yard and didn't see her. She feared her dog may have gotten out somehow, and she prepared to get back in the van to search for her. As she did, she noticed Tasha sitting and staring at an odd patch of dirt in what, hopefully, was planned to become a vegetable garden. "Tasha? TashaKitty? What is it? What are you looking at?" Verna hurried to the cat, looked in the direction of her stare, and saw Questra lying on her side, half concealed under a bush.

"Girl? Questra? What's wrong?" Questra's tail thumped once, but she remained motionless on her side. Verna reached to her and felt her belly was disturbingly distended. Verna pulled her dog out from under the bush, lifted her lip, and saw her gums were nearly white. *Internal bleeding!* Verna rushed into the house, brought out an old blanket to wrap around her dog, placed Questra in the van, and hastened to an emergency vet hospital.

"Ma'am, I'm sorry to tell you this, but she has Parvo Virus. There's nothing I can do. Euthanasia is the kindest course now." The vet smiled as comfortingly as he could and waited. Mutely, numbly, dazedly, Verna nodded her consent. The vet's technician gently took Verna's arm and led her to the reception area where she collapsed, stunned with the awful reality.

When she returned home, Jerry's carpool van had just left, and he had not yet gone into the house. Verna stepped out of the van and sank down to the driveway with grief.

"She died? She had to be put to sleep?" Jerry weaved only slightly and seemed to grasp what had happened. He sat on the gravel next to her. Clumsily, he put an arm around Verna's shoulders. "Oh." He paused as if trying to decide what to say. "Well…She wasn't that good of a dog anyway, was she? I mean…that flopped over ear wasn't exactly pretty, was it?"

Not that good of a dog!? <u>This</u> is your way of consoling me? Damn, Jerry! You insensitive, drooling drunk!

"No, Jerry, she wasn't that good of a dog. She was a <u>great</u> dog! No, her floppy ear wasn't exactly pretty. It was charming and endearing, and I loved her for it. You'll never understand who Questra was, and you'll never understand who I am! And until you can understand loving a dog, you'll never understand loving anything or anybody. And I feel sorry for you, you twisted man, and I pity you in your pathos!"

Verna stood and stomped into the house, leaving Jerry sitting on the coarse gravel with an astonished, wondering look on his face.

Pity me in my pathos? Twisted? What the hell? What was that all about? I need a drink!

Verna ate no supper. Jerry drank his. No word passed between them for the rest of that day.

By May Verna's patience was ended. Yes, she believed in and wanted to honor her wedding vows, just as she had when she first married Patrick. However, as with Patrick's drinking and abuse, she had had enough of Jerry's daily drinking, constant bickering, filthy habits, verbal abuse, and almost psychotic fear of spending money. Her "Era of Marriage to Jerry" had lasted ten years, ten *long*

years which began rather promising as they drove through a misty haze into Seattle, a rare winter's rainbow preceding them. She had not found her pot of gold at the end of that particular rainbow; certainly it hadn't been in their first rental house or the house they purchased at the end of the road. Nor was it anywhere near their house finally built. Anyway, if a pot of gold *had* been in any of those houses, Jerry would probably have hidden the coins away in jars as he hid his trove of quarters in Mason jars behind plywood in the garage of his Tucson house before he and Verna were married in Las Vegas – the same quarters Verna accidentally found which so infuriated Jerry in her finding – the same ones he blew in the slots during their Vegas "honeymoon." No, her pot of gold was not found at the foot of that rainbow followed, and that rainbow dissipated long ago. It was time to look for another one.

While Jerry was at work one day, Verna removed her clothes from her closet, her toiletries from the bathroom, placed Tasha in her wicker carrier, got in the van, drove to an apartment complex, and rented a studio apartment. When Jerry came home, she told him she was filing for divorce. The argument – loud! Verna – adamant! "I've had enough, Jerry. I'm leaving."

"No, by God, you won't! You can't! No…you can't. Uh…um…I'll stop drinking if you'll just stay. I know you don't like it. I can stop. I'll stop. Please. I'll stop drinking." Jerry's eyes pleaded.

"Jerry, you can drink or not drink, that's up to you. You can drink yourself to death if you want to. Do whatever you want to do. I'm doing what *I* want to do now, what I *need* to do, what is best for me now. It's over. I'm not going to keep doing this. I'm leaving you."

Jerry's eyes hardened. "Yeah, well…ok…ok…leavin' are ya?…leavin' me, huh?…where're ya goin'? Huh? Where're ya goin'? What're ya gonna do? Huh? So…I guess yer gonna, what, go to Nashville with that damn stupid guitar an' yer damn stupid songs an' sing, huh? That whatcher gonna do? That where yer plannin' on goin'? Nashville? Singin' songs? No more haulin' papers?" He paused in his tirade. Verna sat, still as a stone, not speaking, allowing Jerry to run down like a wind-up toy monkey clashing cymbals and clamoring gibberish, finally diminishing in slow motion to an exhausted, spent, foolish chatterer.

Jerry turned to the bar with a dismissive wave of his hand. "Yeah, well, go then! Go on! Go the hell on an' play yer damn ol' guitar an' sing yer dumb ol' songs! See if I care! Hell, see if *anybody* cares! I mean, who would wanna listen to a forty-year-old fat lady sing?"

THE FAT LADY SINGS

She stood onstage beside her partner, Norman Levine, in Seattle Center's "Center Stage Area," a huge, two-story, grand room with a platform stage set in its cavernous center. Shops and restaurants lined the perimeters of both lower and upper tiers with protective railings at the edge of the upper tier walkway and escalators at both ends of the room. The area was festively decorated with twinkling lights, wreaths, holly swags from the upper tier railings, and festooned Christmas trees along the lower tier wall. There were about two hundred folding chairs facing the stage, all filled with people. A curtained backdrop shielded the rear of the platform stage. Around the vast room's perimeters were masses of shoppers milling through and around each other like so many ants. There was an undercurrent of shuffling shoppers' feet, mumblings of people talking, and occasional cheery "Merry Christmases" or "Happy Holidays" sounded above the murmuring crowd. It was the beginning of the 1990 Christmas Season, the Seattle Center's annual Season-long "Celebrating Christmas" event, this year kicked off by the professional entertainment team of "The StorySingers." Verna and Norman were in the midst of their original Christmas Show. They began to sing.

And all the milling stopped; all the shuffling ceased; all the mumbling ended. On the top tier, people leaned motionless on the railings, their attention focused on the two performers. The same happened on the lower tier. People stood stationary at escalators without boarding them. Shoppers exiting stores stopped as they stepped into an enchanted moment. All movement throughout the room halted. All noise ceased save for the song Verna and Norman sang in exquisite acapella harmony, its gentle, loving lyrics filling the room through the Center's sound system, ringing loud and clear in amplified splendor, enwrapping everyone in awe-filled silence. It was a song they wrote together, "The Christmas Star," and there was stunned stillness when their last note faded away. It was a magical, mystical, memorable Moment-in-Time, one not long forgotten by those present that day. Verna and Norman stood in the enchantment for silent seconds, then broke the spell as they continued their show, and the milling, shuffling, and mumbling began again.

So who would want to listen to a forty-year-old fat lady sing, now a forty-*four*-year old fat lady who was not fat nor had ever been? In this instance, hundreds wanted to. At this point in her career as a StorySinger, thousands wanted to; thousands had heard her sing. Verna reflected upon Jerry's sarcastic question "Who would want to listen to a forty-year-old fat lady sing?" as she and Norman accepted standing ovation accolades at the end of their show. An elderly, white-haired man stood among those bestowing appreciative acclamations, his rheumy eyes teeming with tears, his chin quivering as he clapped.

Verna thought of how far she had come after Jerry had asked that caustic query in 1986. Memories flooded her – memories of her journey from then till now, four years of memories.

By the time Verna moved away from Jerry and divorced him in May of 1986, he had purchased a car for himself and, in a rare gesture of generosity, signed ownership of the van to Verna as he felt it was hers to use in her work. Shortly after she moved into the apartment complex, she realized it, though a shelter from Jerry, was not the refuge she craved. She needed a quiet, peaceful place to recharge after years of being drained emotionally, a serene space in which she could find herself once more, a silent spot where she could hear the voice of her songs, much like Elijah in his cave heard the still, small voice of God. Surely, as did Elijah, she had experienced great and strong winds – those that rent the mountains of her marriage – earthquakes of emotion, and insane fires of Jerry's fury. It was time to seek solace.

Bill Reilly was one of the numerous realtors she met when she and Jerry fretfully flitted from house to house in their anxious quest to move from that unsuitable rental house in which they first lived in Seattle. He was a kind man, Bill Reilly, a patient, considerate, mindful man. Verna called him. He remembered her. How could he forget the young woman and her "Nervous Nellie" of a worried, fretful husband who agonized over every single aspect of every single house he had once shown them? Yes, he remembered her. He was pleased to hear she was divorced, not for his sake because he was happily married, but for hers.

Bill picked her up at her studio apartment. "I have a place that I think would be perfect for you, Verna! My office will carry the mortgage so you won't need to worry with a bank."

"Oh. Thank you. Thank you very much. So where is it, Bill?" Verna sat on the passenger side of his big Buick. It was practically an antique, but the car was a very smooth ride.

"You'll see. Just relax. I think I've got just the thing you've been looking for."

He smiled as he turned onto a small rise, and Verna saw rows of manufactured homes. "Oh, no, not a trailer! I really don't want to live in a trailer park, Bill." Verna's disappointment was quite evident.

"See, this here is all adults." He gestured out his side window. "It's an adults-only park. And just look. Flowers. Everywhere."

The big car slowly drove through the entrance pillars, around a curve and up another rise to the top of a hill. A pond came into view. "Look. There's even a blue heron that comes here to fish. And see the ducks? Makes ya feel restful just to watch 'em swim around, don't it? And back there right behind the park is a green belt. No noise. No traffic. No kids yelling. Just peaceful."

Verna looked. It really was a beautiful spot. Flowers. Pond. Trees. Quiet. Peaceful. But still…*a trailer?* She shook her head. "I dunno…never pictured a…a *trailer*…Y'know?"

"Well, just wait till you see this one. It has everything you need, and…it's gonna be well within your budget. You'll be able to get a new van with the money you'll save."

Hmmm…well, I <u>do</u> need a new van. The old one of Jerry's has a lot of wear and tear on it, and it is getting tired.

Bill parked in the carport of a single-wide manufactured home on top of the hill at the very back end of the park next to the greenbelt. The pond was directly across from it with no other home in front. There were only two other homes on its right side, and the greenbelt butted up to its rear. The location was relatively isolated from other manufactured homes "down the hill," and this home was the perfect size for a single woman and her cat. It was indeed the refuge of serenity for which she searched, a harbor from the harsh hubbub of the newspaper warehouse, and a retreat in which to restore herself once more. Though she had no way of knowing, it was one of the places prepared through those "Mysterious Ways" for her to meet one of her greatest "Wonders," the true love of her life.

Bill arranged the appropriate papers. She signed. She moved into the last place she would live in Seattle.

The Seattle Times spotters unionized, and Verna carried a Teamster's card. She made $16.95 an hour plus mileage, good wages in 1986. She bought a new, sleek, black Ford van, the very first vehicle she had ever picked out just for herself. It had a magnificent sound system, which, to her, was its most important feature. It also had no vestiges of Questra's presence, no memories of her beloved dog embedded in its upholstery. Plus there were no "remnants of Jerry" in this van. It was a new symbol of her new life! Driving delivery runs was as second nature to her now as playing her guitar. She was now a trainer of new hires, and she gladly dispensed her wisdom to help them settle in.

Verna often pondered the unexpected Life Path she'd walked from a high school veterinarian's assistant, to wife and mother, Welfare Ironing Lady, nursing student, an LPN trained as an OR Nurse, a private duty caregiver, a catatonic patient in a mental hospital, a valuable assistant in a Seattle Veterinary practice, and now a Teamster in a Seattle Times warehouse driving a new van with sureness and confidence – a Teamster who was also becoming a consummate musician and songwriter. It was a most unique Path she walked, one filled with past and present miracles, one on which she was guided and sustained by her deep Christian faith, for how else could her overcomings be explained except by God's Guidance?

Father, where are You taking me now? You have walked with me through so many twists and turns and have pulled me out of so many pits of despair. Thank you, God. Where are You taking me now?

Wherever God was taking her, she felt she would stay with The Times. It was good pay. She remained in touch with Doctor Griffin of the Aurora Veterinary Clinic where she worked when she and Jerry first moved to Seattle. It was good to have backup. *Yes, if I ever lose my job at The Times, I can always go back to the veterinary clinic as an assistant.* Ah, but "Homo proponit, sed Deus disponit," as the 15th century German cleric, Thomas a Kempis, wrote in his book "The Imitation of Christ" – "Man proposes, but God disposes."

Verna continued to dream of her daughters. She maintained the method of communication with Susanna via exchange of letters through her friend Janice in Tucson. Perhaps the "secretiveness" of it appealed to the little girl. Certainly she missed her mother. With attention focused on Veronica as a runaway and on her baby sister as a "miracle child," Susanna needed continual contact with Verna, as secretively sporadic as it was. Thus, Verna received hand-drawn pictures, school photos, letters scrawled in a childish hand, and reports of grades earned. She was thrilled to receive the letter about Susanna's baptism. She kept Susanna's letters in a binder, and her return letters always included scriptural references and reminders her daughter was loved. Verna longed for communication from Veronica.

One afternoon, as she pulled into her carport, she heard her telephone ringing. "Hello?"

"Mom? Mom? Will you come get me? Please?" A young girl's voice!

Verna's heart nearly stopped. She caught the breath whooshing out of her and said, "Of course, Honey. Of course I'll come and get you." Adrenaline surged through every cell as relief flooded through her system. That breath she caught became a sob, and she was barely able to whisper, "Tell me where you are, Honey."

…Silence…

"Where *are* you? I'll be right there. Just tell me where you are, Sweetheart!"

"…Uh…I'm at the bowling alley…with Jennifer and Dolores…but we finished early…"

Whoooomp! What little breath Verna had left was completely knocked out of her. *This girl is not Veronica!* It took a moment to reassamble herself. She couldn't let tears come or she would dissolve in a cataract of them. Finally able to breathe again, she mustered the strongest, steadiest voice she could and replied, "Um…I'm afraid you've called the wrong number. You have reached Verna Hansen."

"…Oh…sorry…" *click*

Verna hung up. Her legs buckled as she slid down the wall onto the floor.

Wracked with sobs, she wept bitter tears. Tasha came to her, curled up in her lap, kneaded her with soft paws, and offered the best feline comfort she could. Verna sat on the floor of her manufactured home's small kitchen with its harvest gold refrigerator and range, sobbed profusely, and petted the dear cat who had come so serendipitously into her life. Tasha was no ZipperCat, the wonderful black cat she had in Orlando, and she certainly was no Questra. But she was her cat, and Verna took comfort from the warm, purring, furry presence in her lap.

Now, once again single, Verna "church hunted." She found and joined a large, non-denominational, downtown Seattle Christian church, simply and serendipitously named "The Way." *Father, have You brought me to The Way through one of Your Mysterious Ways? What Wonder will be worked here, Dear God?*

She loved the church. The congregation called it the "Seven-Eleven of Churches" since it offered so many events. It featured a hundred-voice volunteer choir, Wednesday night light suppers, various programs every weeknight, three Sunday morning services at 8, 10 and 11, and a Sunday evening Vespers service at 6:00pm. Fellowship time with refreshments happened between services. Quite often people would stay for every service. When the main sanctuary filled, an overflow space was available in the church library, the service broadcast on speakers. Cassette tapes of every service were provided. Verna had never experienced anything like it.

As she did years ago in Orlando's Oak Creek United Methodist church, she became Sunday School teacher for toddlers, ages potty-trained to 5 years. As she once named her class in Orlando, she dubbed her Seattle class her "Sunshine Kids." Once again she used music to inspire the young ones as she played Michelle in Sunday School. Once more she taught joy songs to children, and once more her children's choir taught the congregation to sing as children sing, as her "Sunshine Choir" did long ago in Oak Creek Methodist. Now with a guitar, she taught Bible stories with a flannel board and Sunday School songs with guitar accompaniment. She was in her element.

Now living alone, Verna could practice her guitar as well as write and sing her songs to her heart's content. Songs surfaced from dreams or from wakeful inspirations, and she kept paper and pen close by to capture them. *Songs come from the heart…from the deepest heart of a person…that's where music lives… that's where my music lives!*

Verna wrote many songs. She *had* to write them, to play them, to sing them – was compelled to do so. It was as if her inspirational floodgates opened. Many times songs came unbidden. Sometimes she awakened hearing them. Other times she sat with pen and paper, wrote lyrics as fast as they flooded her mind, picked up Michelle, and fitted melody and chords to words. To her it was always a mystical process, as, indeed, creative processes are. She bought a small tape recorder to record her songs, play them back, sing along with them, and harmonize with herself. It was an entirely new world for her. She discovered things about herself she never suspected. Her dad used to say she was practically born singing, and songs surrounded her as her family sang. Yet no one in her family ever actually "created" songs. Oh, sometimes family members might make up silly words to known melodies. This was not that, though. What was happening now was different. Verna, herself, originated lyrics, melodies, chords, and strum patterns; she was the vessel to which and through which they came. She was once more in the midst of one of God's Mysterious Ways, a Way that began when she plunged into catatonia only to be led out through singing "Amazing Grace" and a guitar placed around her neck. She, completely oblivious to her unknown future, was being prepared for one of God's Greatest Wonders. She was amid an overcoming of her old life – all of it – and being born anew like a butterfly emerges as a new creature from its former life. Her cocoon was unraveling, strand by strand, song by song.

Thank You, Father, for giving me this gift...thank You for helping me through all this!

One fateful afternoon Verna was given a packet to take to The Times' downtown Seattle corporate office. She approached the receptionist. "Hi, I'm Verna Hansen, a spotter at Lake City Warehouse. I'm supposed to deliver this to Ned Flatt."

"Thank you, Ms. Hansen. You may leave it with me, and I'll be certain he gets it."

She left it with the receptionist at the front desk and turned to go. A man standing near called to her, "Hold up there a sec. I'll be right with you." Then he was at her side, reaching to shake her hand.

"Hi. I'm Gary Gerdes. I'm one of the new regional managers here. I want to ride along with a spotter tomorrow. Is it okay if I ride with you?" His grin was wide and boyish, but his eyes, behind his glasses, were serious. All business.

"Sure. That would be fine, Mr. Gerdes. I'll be at Lake City Distribution Center tomorrow at eleven. See you then."

Verna turned and left. She had no way of knowing she had just met the man who would produce her first demo tape.

The next day, sitting in her van, attired in shirt, tie, blue sweater and navy slacks, Gary looked for all the world like a college boy. He asked numerous questions about all aspects of spotters' duties, and Verna answered them with good humor. He offered to help unload bundles, but she told him to keep his seat. The delivery run completed, she headed back to the warehouse. She asked if he'd mind if she played some music, and he nodded. She put in her tape, home-produced on her small tape recorder; her voice and guitar sprang forth from the speakers. Gary's head snapped around.

"Who is that? Who is that singer?" He peered at her over his glasses.

Verna chuckled self-consciously. "Well…that's me. I'll turn it off if you like. These songs are just me sitting in front of a little tape recorder." She reached for the "OFF" switch, but he held his hand over hers in restraint.

"No. Please. I'd really like to listen." He increased the volume. "Little Girl Gone" unfurled from the speakers like an audible banner, and Verna sang with the song, harmonizing with herself. Next came "Rainbows on the Ground," a bouncy song she wrote for Susanna, based on a day after an Orlando rainstorm when they searched together for rainbows, and the little girl found one in a parking lot's oily puddle. Gary stared at her in a disconcertingly direct way. "You sing! And you wrote these songs?" Verna nodded. "Wow! You have a wonderful voice!"

Gary Gerdes was also a musician – a musician with a complete home recording studio – a musician who wanted to generate professionally-produced demo tapes for Verna. In his studio he augmented her guitar with accompanying instruments on his synthesizer, and she sang layers of harmony with herself. The end result was astonishing! It was the conception of a new career, a turn she would soon take on the Pathway on which she walked, a coming-of-age of her childhood singing as she and her "grownups" sat on their rural Oklahoma front porch and "sang the sun down."

"Verna, I didn't know you played guitar!" Joseph Couch saw the guitar case neck protruding above the top of the van's passenger seat as he helped load her bundles. He grinned and tossed in the last one. "You've been holding out on me, young lady!"

"Well, I'm sorta learning on my own. Never had lessons or anything. I just play chords and sing the song. I don't play the melody on the guitar."

"Neither does Johnny Cash," chuckled Joe. Both he and Verna were fans. "I sure would like to hear you play sometime. I'll talk to Jean and let's have you come by for dinner soon, okay? And you could bring your guitar." He paused a moment as if debating about asking a question. Verna waited expectantly. "Does your guitar have a name? BB King calls his 'Lucille.' Even buys it a plane ticket so it can be in the seat next to him when he travels."

"Michelle. My guitar's name is Michelle." Verna slid into the driver's seat and smiled at Joe's reflection in the rear-view mirror. "Sure thing, Joe. Dinner would be great." He closed the rear doors and thumped them twice to signal the vehicle was ready to go.

Verna sang her songs all through the day, harmonizing with herself on her tape. During breaks between loadings at the distribution center, she sat in her van, played, and sang. And smiled. A lot.

Verna enjoyed a wonderful meal at Joe and Jean Couch's house, a lovely dinner of seared cod, aspaaragus, and glazed baby carrots. Joe and Jean were fisher folk, and they always kept their freezer filled with fish. Their high school-aged son, CJ, was fascinated to hear that Verna played guitar and had actually written songs!

"I'm learning to play bass at school. Maybe sometime I could play bass with you." His eyes shone.

"That would be lovely, CJ. I know nothing about the bass, and, actually, I know precious little about the guitar. Another guitarist showed me basic chords once upon a time, and I've learned others along the way. And, as far as strum patterns go, I just kinda do what I feel the song needs."

Jean poured coffee to take into the living room. "So…when are you going to leave us and go to Nashville and become a star, Verna?" She smiled and handed Verna her cup.

Verna suddenly felt self-conscious. "Oh, I only play in church. For my Sunday School class, or for Vacation Bible School. Never played in front of an actual audience of grownups. Not for real, anyway. It's pretty doubtful that Dolly Parton or Reba McIntryre need fear any threat from me." Verna grinned an embarrassed grin.

They passed a pleasant evening in front of the fireplace, Verna presenting songs she'd recently written. Her friends exuded compliments. They were Christians, as was she, so they sang through all the old gospel songs they knew, and, if Verna could play them on the guitar, she did. Otherwise, they sang without guitar accompaniment. CJ had the time of his life. So did Verna.

Jean brought out an apple crisp for dessert and asked Verna about her song "Little Girl Gone." "You have children, Verna?" She dished ice cream into bowls and paused, seeming to stare intently at her.

Somehow it made her very uncomfortable to discuss this, so Verna briefly replied, "Yes. Daughters. They live with my ex and his wife in Tucson." She didn't mention the baby she'd given up for adoption, although in her heart that baby, her "Chrissy," was also one of her daughters and always would be. "My oldest, Veronica, ran away from home. I dream of her, you see, and the song came in a dream." Jean went back to the kitchen.

"Wow! A whole song just…came out of a dream? That's crazy good!" CJ slurped his ice cream.

"Yeah. Crazy good," echoed Verna.

MIRACLES OCCUR NATURALLY –
WE JUST HAVE TO PAY ATTENTION

Verna recorded several sessions in Gary Gerdes' studio and now played her demo tape in her van as she sang along with herself. She sent one to Janice and Derek and one to her mother and Robert. Her mother was thrilled. In a phone conversation, Arlene asked if she and Robert could help her "get her music out," as in shop the Demo around to music producers. Verna declined, saying it was enough to have the tape to listen to herself. She hoped one day to send one to Susanna. And, hopefully, Veronica would return to them and she could also hear her song, "Little Girl Gone."

"Hey, Gary, how are ya?" Verna entered his studio, set down Michelle, and removed her coat. "I've got a new song. Came just this week! I was in the grocery store getting ready to check out, when I saw long lines at every single register, so I decided to stop in the refreshment area and get a Coke and wait it out. And now I've got a new song. Just wait'll you hear it!" Verna beamed, and pulled crumpled pieces of paper from her pocket to lay on the music stand. "I wrote on napkins." She unlatched the guitar case, removed her beloved Michelle, and placed the strap around her neck. "Listen, this is how it goes." Verna downstrummed into the opening verse.

"Whatcha used ta get for a nickel...sells for a quarter today...what used ta sell two for a quarter...ya pay a dollar anyway..."

Gary flicked on the mic because he often liked to capture these impromptu moments. There was a sort of magic there that might not be present in subsequent tracks. When she finished, he asked, "What key are you playing in, Verna?"

"Uh...Key of G, I guess. It starts on the G chord." She lifted her eyebrows in query. "Something wrong?"

"No, not really, but it felt to me as if you were singing in a low register, and it might sound better if you sang it a little higher, like, maybe in the key of C?" As he talked, Gary fiddled with the controls on his soundboard.

Verna pinkened a bit, embarrassed. "Uh...well, actually I can't play in the Key of C. It's because of the F chord in that progression. It's a bar chord, and, well, I just can't do bar chords." She shrugged.

"Ah. I see. Well, let me introduce you to...a capo!" He removed something from his pocket and reached for her guitar. "May I?" He fastened the little gadget on the fretboard in the fifth fret. "Now, strum a G Chord."

As Verna did so, her eyebrows went up. "What just happened?"

"The capo changes the pitch of the strings. When you place a capo on the guitar neck five frets up from the G Chord, you are now playing in the Key of C. Try it. Do the whole song."

Verna did. She was playing the same chords she knew, but it was now higher, and easier to sing. "Wow! Gary I had no idea...no clue that was even possible."

He chuckled softly. "Well, now you know. So what's the name of this one, 'Two for a Quarter?' Or do you have something else in mind?"

"Well, that's what I thought it was, at first, but no, I think the name of it is 'Memories' because of the first line in the chorus.

"...I like memories...they tickle my fancy still…best of all about memories...I can pick and choose at will...the good ones I can review...the sad ones leave behind...the ones that are the goodest…are the happy kind..."

"Memories it is. Let's lay some tracks. Do you like that key? You can change it, you know. Just place the capo somewhere else on the neck."

As Gary set up his recording equipment, he told Verna that Irving Berlin, famous composer of the Christmas classic "White Christmas," only played keyboard in the Key of C, so he had a specially made piano with a lever where he could change the pitch of the strings, much as a capo changes the pitch on guitar strings. Verna's song was done in one take.

Gary also introduced Verna to finger picks as well as a wood block designed to amplify an acoustic guitar. Basically self-taught, Verna developed her own unique method of guitar playing. She picked it quite similarly as a banjo player picks a banjo, and it was stunningly amazing. From her first hesitant strum on Tom Nation's guitar in Mesquite Valley Mental Hospital's Musical Therapy Night – the night in which "Amazing Grace" reached deep into her darkness of catatonia to take her psyche's hand and lead her to light once more – Verna ripened into an accomplished, skillful, talented guitarist whose singular style was mesmerizing. She would thrill thousands in years yet to come. Ecclesiastes famously states "To everything there is a season." Verna's season was coming upon her as she was entering her "time to be born," her "time to plant" for she was indeed planting seeds in her soul which would mature in their "time to pluck up that which is planted."

Verna was becoming a new person, finally growing into a person she really liked. Her heartaches were still there, but, like an oyster encapsulates a grain of sand with layers of nacre and makes it into a pearl, so her heartaches were cushioned by layers of prayer. Finally coming to understand she could not will herself to find her daughters while dreaming, she would simply settle herself for sleep with her cat, Tasha, close by, and jot down dreams in her dream journal. She dreamed of Veronica, her eldest, relatively often, sometimes blowing gently on her cheek as if to say, "I'm here...I'm here with you." Occasionally, her eldest would reach and touch her cheek as if wondering what that was. These dreams convinced Verna that Veronica was alive and they would reunite one day. It had been awhile since she'd heard from Susanna, but she wrote letters every week to Janice who took them to Susanna's schoolyard and gave them to her.

Dearest Susanna,

Thank you for your last letter. I'm so happy that our friend, Janice, is helping us this way so we can write each other. I am sorry for asking you to deceive Daddy and Mommy Anne Marie, but I miss you so. Congratulations on such good grades! I am so very proud of you!

I am doing well. My job keeps me really busy. I drive a van in Seattle traffic, delivering bundles of newspapers to carriers all over King County. I do enjoy being outside, even if it is chilly and damp and rains most of the time. I've learned to love the rain.

Recently, I got a new cat. Her owners took her to the vet hospital to be spayed, but didn't come back to get her. When I met her, I just knew she was my cat, and somehow she knew I was her person. Came straight into my arms and purred. Her name is Tasha. She is a tabby-point Siamese. That means her body is a light cream color, and her ears, paws, and tail are black and gray striped like a tabby cat. She is just the sweetest thing. She is nowhere as bouncy and energetic as our Zipper cat was; I guess you'd say she is more of a lap cat.

I'm learning to play the guitar better. I practice every day. The first song I ever wrote was about your sister, and the very next song I wrote was about you. You were very little so you probably don't remember, but in Florida one day there was a fierce thunderstorm, and the noise scared you and you cried and cried. So I told you the story of old Father Noah and the ark in the Bible, and promised you and I would go find a rainbow when the rain stopped and we did. You found the first one in an oily puddle. And then a rainbow appeared in the sky. It's a pretty song. I'll sing it for you one day. It's called "Rainbows on the Ground."

Love, Mommy Verna

The single-wide manufactured home was the perfect refuge. It was paneled in pine paneling, which actually made for lovely acoustics. Verna would crank open the windows and sit at her small kitchen table with pen, paper, and guitar and play to her heart's content. She had a television, but rarely watched it, much preferring to play her guitar or read. She often wondered what this all meant. While she did play and sing for the kids in her Sunday School class, she didn't perform anywhere else. And she didn't feel her music was "in sync" with what other musicians created. Hers was uniquely her own. She loved the process even though she didn't understand it. It was as if a colorful kite had appeared in her sky, she had caught its bright tail, and was now soaring through melodies and lyrics practically at will. The kite pulled on her constantly, and it was exhilarating.

The year waned, and fall was upon them. Fall in the Pacific Northwest was as colorful as spring. Blazing colors of orange, red, yellow, brown, and russet appeared everywhere; vivid leaves carpeted the ground like crackling confetti dropped upon a parade of days marching to 1987. It would be warm enough to wear a tee shirt one day, and chilly enough for a jacket the next. Verna kept both in her van in an "emergency" cardboard box. She practically lived in her vehicle as did the other spotters. Tab was her drink of preference, and she bought it by the case. She also had a huge stainless thermos and carried coffee with her. She kept a variety of granola bars and similar snacks in her van as there was not always time for a real meal break.

It was Labor Day. Verna attended many evening classes and Bible study groups at her church, so often didn't get home until late at night. After her day's delivery run of newspaper bundles, she went out to eat and then to church for her usual Monday night discussion group, "One is a Whole Number," a dialogue on surviving divorce. When she returned home, the living room was a mess. She smelled feces and urine. Tasha, appearing unconscious, lay stretched on her side in the middle of the carpet.

"Tasha? TashaKitty?" Verna knelt down next to the sweet little cat, and she lifted her head at Verna's touch. The expression in her eyes was one of puzzlement as if she weren't sure where she was. Carefully Verna scooped her up and sat on the settee with her in her lap. She stroked the furry head. Suddenly the cat's back arched, and she began jerking spasmodically. A grand mal seizure! "Oh, no, TashaKitty. Oh, dear."

The next morning Verna took Tasha to Doctor Griffin's hospital. She knew he was often in early, and, sure enough, there were lights on when she arrived. She knocked on the back door, Tasha in her wicker carrier. "It's me. Verna. Please, Doctor Griffin, it's Tasha."

"Goodness, Verna, what in the world...?" His eyes were very round, seeing tears on her cheeks.

"She's having seizures. She's been having them all night. I got home late, see, after my class at church, and she looked like she'd been having seizures for hours. The living room's a mess."

Gently, Verna tipped the carrier up and reached in for Tasha. She started seizing. Verna held her gently on the table. Doctor Griffin looked in her eyes with a penlight. One pupil was larger than the other. Verna looked at him with hope. "Is there anything you can do? Anything?"

He laid his hand on Verna's arm, and looked her in the eye. "I'm so sorry, Verna. This looks like a brain tumor. I'm afraid there's nothing I can do."

Tasha mewed once, very softly, and started seizing again. "Let me do it, Doctor Griffin. Please. Let me help her cross the Rainbow Bridge." Verna looked pleadingly at him.

"No, Verna. It will be best if I do it. You just hold her. Talk to her. I don't think she can see, but she'll know your voice." He busied himself with the syringe.

Verna held the exhausted cat against her breast and spoke soothingly in her ear, stroking her head.

It was over quickly, and Tasha's body went limp. Doctor Kurtzmann came in just then, took her arm, and helped her into the office where she could sit. He handed her tissues. They talked for some time. "Verna, you gave her the best home. The best life. She loved you. Had it not been for you, she would have had to go to a shelter to be euthanized as an unwanted cat. You were a big blessing to her."

"She was a big blessing to me, too. After I left Jerry, it was just me and Tasha, y'know?" Verna sniffled into a fresh tissue. "I nearly died when I heard my daughter ran away. I nearly died again when I had to euthanize Questra. And now...now...TashaKitty." She sobbed on the vet's shoulder.

"Well, just remember, when God closes one door, it means another is about to open. The way is being prepared for the next chapter in your life. Perhaps it's something which is for you to do alone. No husband. No children. No pets. Who knows what the future brings. So there is no way to prepare for it except to follow God's path as He lays it out for us." He stood and helped Verna up. Taking her hand in his, he smiled at her gently. "You will be all right, my dear. You don't know it now, but you will be okay." He turned toward the door and Doctor Griffin was there to walk her to the van. He put a gentle arm around her shoulders for a moment. "Verna, we're here. Please let us help you. If you need us we're only a phone call away." He smiled and waved as she backed out.

Fall gave way to winter. Verna made her usual Christmas preparations, sent out her Christmas cards, sent a birthday card to Children's Home Society of Florida for Chrissy, made her handcrafted gifts, and took twenty five lap robes to a neighborhood senior center as gifts for the residents. The Director invited her to come and sing carols, so she took Michelle and led the group in the Day Room in Christmas carols. It was the first time she ever played in front of an audience. Surprisingly, she found herself quite at home. Maybe all those Sunday School classes were paying off. The staff thanked her profusely, and several residents hugged her while seated in their wheelchairs.

She couldn't attend Christmas Eve service due to having to work, but she went to the Christmas morning service when she finished her last delivery run. In the new "Women Only" bathroom in the warehouse, she changed from jeans to a long black velvet skirt, white blouse, nylons, and heels, earning a chorus of long low whistles from men she considered teammates. One man called out, "Hey Vern...you look like a...like a...girl!" At that, Paulie grinned, and said, "No sir, that's no girl. That's a woman right there!" Verna smiled prettily, batted her eyes, thanked them, and left for church. Afterward she went to Joe and Jean Couch's for Christmas morning. After gifts were exchanged and the turkey was in the oven, she became sleepy since she had worked all Christmas Eve night. They invited her to sleep in their guest room. As she slept, she dreamed.

Verna ran across a grassy meadow. Her movements awkward due to the long skirt she wore, but she was very happy. Blitz, her German shepherd puppy from her girlhood, joyfully caught a ball and ran back to her with it in his mouth. Then she felt a playful nudge in her side and looked down. It was Questra, with her charming flop ear and big doggy grin. She petted both beautiful dogs and started to cry. As she did so, she felt a weight on her shoulder and heard a familiar purr. It was her black cat, Zipper, from when she lived in Orlando. When she left there, she placed him in the care of her friend and landlord, Mr. Jennie, and now he joined her in her dream, walking beside her. She picked up the ball to throw it again for Blitz and went to sit on a gray boulder, as she did, she realized Tasha was there, her coloring and markings blending perfectly with the stone. She meowed quietly in welcome, just as she had in life. Verna sat, Mr. Jennie beside her, Zipper perched on her shoulder with Tasha purring in her lap, and enjoyed a mild breeze, the green meadow, and the company of her former pets and land-lord. "How are ya, Verna?" Mr. Jennie asked.

"Well..."

The dream shifted, and she floated over treetops, seeking her daughter. There. Off to the right. A wisp of smoke. A campfire? She drifted toward it, having no more substance than smoke herself. Veronica's voice wafted toward her. There was indeed a small campfire ringed with stones, Veronica and an older man seated on the ground beside it with three dogs – the smooth- coated brindle, the big brown-and-white fluffy one, and a small black-and-white terrier tucked inside the man's partially-zipped jacket. The weather was cold and the two were dressed in many layers of clothing, Verna noted, with a black-and-red plaid wool jacket topping off the man's wardrobe. Veronica, a blue bandanna covering her hair, was dressed all in denim. Jeans, vest, and jacket. Both appeared to be quite comfortable.

"So, Walt. What did you get me for Christmas?" Veronica grinned and sipped from a steaming mug in her hand. A blue enamel coffee pot sat in the midst of the fire and burbled to itself.

"Do I look like ol' Santy Claus to you? Ain't got no red hat. Ain't got no sled and no deer, do I?" The man's whiskered face softened into a smile. Verna saw he had no front teeth.

"Nope, I don't reckon you do, at that," grinned Veronica. "I got you sump'n though. Just a sec." She rummaged in her backpack next to her on the ground. Verna thought it extraordinary. It was fashioned from faded denim, and appeared to be handmade. Nearly every inch was embroidered with all manner of designs – spirals, stars, a crescent moon, stick figures of people, a hand. It was actually quite a work of art. Veronica zipped it closed, and said, "Now close your eyes and I'll give you a nice surprise." Walt closed his eyes. She placed something in his hands.

"Wal, looky there! That's ol' Jim! You know I like ol' Jim when I c'n get 'im!" He grinned toothlessly. "Thankee, Ronnie. 'at's mighty thoughtful of ya."

Verna saw a bottle of Jim Beam whisky. "Now, that ain't for just drinkin'. That's for keepin'. That's for when ya feel the shakes comin' on. Think of it like... like...medicine. Okay?" Veronica clapped him on the shoulder and said, "Merry Christmas!"

Walt stirred and unzipped his own pack. "Achally...I do got sumpn' for ya, but it didn't come from the North Pole, and it warn't made by no elves. Sumpn' I think you'll like..." He rummaged for a bit. "Now it's yore turn. Close yore eyes, cuz you gonna git a nice s'prise." Gently, almost with reverence, he placed a tattered paperback book in her hands. "Wow! Walt! Thank you!" She turned it over. "'The Call of the Wild,' by Jack London," she said with an almost childlike glee. "Oh, Walt! It's a favorite. I haven't read it in a long time. I love it!"

"Yer welcome. Now I know I c'n jus' go ta sleep, cuz there won't be nuthin' more outta ya fer tha rest-a tha day." He cackled a good natured laugh and stretched out on the ground, hugging his bottle, and the small terrier.

Veronica sat, cross legged, the book already open on her lap. Absently, she tossed another stick of wood in the small fire. Verna blew gently on a page causing it to riffle and move slightly. With irritation, Veronica held it down and kept her eyes on the words. Verna blew again, this time at Veronica's cheek, causing a wisp of silky light brown hair to come loose from the bandana. Veronica left it alone, attention riveted on her book.

"Verna...Dinner's ready," Jean called from the closed door. Verna started surfacing from her dream, lying on the plaid bedspread of the twin bed in the Couch's guest room, still in her long skirt and white blouse. A tear escaped and rolled down her temple. She swiped it away. "Coming. Be right there." Had any of that been real? Was her daughter actually camped in the woods on Christmas

Day with three dogs and an older man named Walt? Once home she would record the dream in her journal.

It was Wednesday, December 31, 1986 – New Year's Eve. Verna, though tired from work, was determined to attend the Watchnight Service at church. The special feature of "The Way's Watchnight" was praying in the New Year. In the still silence, the minister, Samuel Furman, led them into prayer as the organist softly played an old hymn, "God's Way Is Best." *How appropriate that is,* thought Verna as the Refrain played in her mind. *God's way is best, I will not murmur although the end I may not see; where'er He leads I'll meekly follow, God's way is best, is best for me.*

"And now...we join God in stillness as the old year passes and the New Year is born...we thank Thee, Heavenly Father, for all the blessings we received and the many lessons we learned...we greet this new year with joy as we follow Your Way, and we know we shall find You ever present for wherever we go, there You are, with us on our mountaintops, with us in our deepest depths...we know You are here with us now, filling this room, around us, beside us, within us…we quiet our minds as we go into our inner closet to meet You, shutting out all cares, all concerns, all thoughts but thoughts of You…quietly we meet You, Father…quietly we allow ourselves to fall into Your embrace…to be alone with You…in the silent time." The organist tapered the hymn to silence as the last chord reverberated away. "Now we pray in the quietness and peace of our hearts...as we meet God alone, sharing our souls, sorrows, and joys with Him, listening in the silence for His still, small voice to show us the way…His Way...alone with God…"

An absolute hush descended in the vast church. Small sounds could be heard. Someone shifting position. An occasional rustle. A soft shushing from a mother to a babe. Someone yawned. Muffled coughs sounded here and there. Yet there was stillness. There was spirit moving in the air. There was sacred space filling the sanctuary, enveloping everyone in a mystic holiness that tingled one's very skin. After some time passed, the organ began again, faintly, gradually increasing in volume, leading the congregation back to an outer awareness. The choir softly sang "God's way is best. I will not murmur although the end I may not see. Where'er He leads I'll meekly follow. God's way is best, is best for me."

"And so may it be. Amen! May the Lord make His face to shine upon you and grant you peace!" Reverend Furman raised his hand in benediction. "Please stand and join me in singing the Peace Song." The familiar chords rang out, as the people joined hands and sang, "Let there be peace on earth and let it begin with me...let there be peace on earth...the peace that was meant to be...with God as our Father...Brothers all are we...let us walk with each other...in perfect harmony..."

Verna joined in with full voice. *I need to learn this on the guitar...I like this song...* As the song crescendoed to a close, she felt her heart open. She carried so much grief and sadness within her that it was as if it were a palpable weight. As her heart opened, she felt it lighten.

"Happy New Year, Verna!" She heard a familiar voice in the hubbub. "You staying for the dancing?" It was Reed Evans, the facilitator for the discussion group "One is a Whole Number."

"Dancing? Where?" Verna's eyes widened.

"Downstairs in the Fellowship Hall. You didn't know?" Reed smiled his wide, generous smile. He was a very handsome black man, bald pate shiny, curly goatee on his chin bobbed as he spoke. "Yeah. Everybody brings tapes and records and you can play whatever you like, dance if you feel like it. Dance with a friend. Dance by yourself. Heck, we'll probably get some line dancing in, too, and maybe even do a Conga line all through the church later. Wanna go out front, though, and see the Space Needle? They light it up real special on New Year's Eve."

Together Verna and Reed stood outside in the crowd at the front of the church, all looking up at the Space Needle. As lights rippled and played on the tall thin spire, Verna felt something. It was as if she were standing in a rushing wind, only the night was still. Fireworks could be heard all over the city as people celebrated the new year, but, for Verna, it was as if something were being celebrated inside her. It was quite odd, this feeling. Maybe God was blowing on *her* cheek as she blew on her daughters' in dreams? *What's that scripture about all being in one place and suddenly a rushing wind came?*

"Reed? Do you feel that?"

"Feel what?" asked the tall black man beside her gazing up at the Space Needle.

"I dunno. A sort of...wind, maybe? Only it's inside?" The lights reflected in Verna's eyes as she looked up.

"Oh. That. Well, I reckon you're feeling the miracle. It's the miracle of the new year. Nineteen Eighty Seven. A clean slate. Blank pages to write your next chapters on. Feels different for everybody. To you, I guess it feels like wind. A wind inside you. That's God blowin' you a miracle." He smiled down at her. "Miracles occur naturally. You just gotta pay attention. Let's dance."

"One dance, Reed. I gotta get home and get some sleep. I can get in at least six hours before I gotta go back to work. Let's dance to the miracle God's blowin' my way."

It *was* a miracle wafting her way. Perhaps she indeed felt the Breath of God blowing on her cheek, a "Divine Rushing Wind" whooshing away her inner constraints for she was close to opening her very being to a Great Wonder for which she was being prepared.

Yet...another apparent misfortune was also in the wind.

GOING THE WRONG WAY CAN
LEAD TO THE RIGHT ONE

The winter of 1987 was one of the worst in Seattle's history. A severe seven-inch snowstorm in January created near total white-out, true blizzard conditions that literally "stopped the city in its tracks." Strong, swirling winds so ferociously whooshed snow mixed with ice pellets that flakes felt like shotgun blasts of small, hard bbs upon one's bare skin. Interestingly, before April 23, 1870, the term "blizzard" actually described a volley of musket fire. It was on that date when an Estherville, Iowa newspaper described a severe snowstorm as a "blizzard," the whooshing winds whizzing iced snowflakes like multitudes of musket balls zipping through the air. Seattle's storm was the same on this day 117 years after Estherville's "Northern Vindicator" first described a "blizzard" in print. By whatever name this particular Seattle snowstorm was called, it was bone-chillingly cold, blindingly white, and ragingly, roaringly windy. In short, it was hazardous! Extremely! Yet, as was true when Mount St. Helens blew apart, raining its own blizzard of choking, clogging ash upon the city, The Seattle Times would be delivered! As the U.S. Postal Service's motto states, "Neither snow nor rain nor heat nor gloom of night stays these couriers from the swift completion of their appointed rounds," The Seattle Times spotters and carriers also will not be stayed from *their* completions. Although one "appointed round" was not completed swiftly this freezing, stormy, snowy night.

Verna, a wool muffler around her neck, a double-layer woolen cap on her head, and wearing her waterproof Goretex coat and boots, loaded her van, drove into the storm, and delivered bundles to her carriers. Her entire van, including the windshield and rearview mirrors, quickly coated in ice. The van, cumbrous with its ice coat, became sluggish, responded slowly to turning or braking, and heavily rocked in gusting winds. She could only drive safely at a snail's pace with her head out the window, since she couldn't see through the thickly iced windshield, yet she was nearly blinded by blowing snow, ice crusting on her eyebrows, her eyes stinging from the cold. She pulled into a service station to put on tire chains. The attendant offered, "Hey, I'll do that for ya for ten bucks." "You're on, pal. Thanks."

With chained tires gripping better, she drove more confidently yet still laboriously slowly. Her last run of the night finally done, she returned to the warehouse, thoroughly cold and very tired. Gary Lawson was lead that weekend.

Cigarette in hand he said, "Sure looks rough out there. Glad to see you. Didja see Robert Graves' van while you were out?" He peered out the breakroom window as if expecting to see him drive up. "He ain't back yet."

"Nope. I didn't see him. I was on Morningside. I think he drew Laurelhurst tonight." She yawned and turned to go.

"Well, stick aroun' a bit. If he ain't back inna half hour ya gotta go look fer 'im. You know tha rule. Last one in looks fer tha lost." Gary looked at her with almost a glare in his eyes as if expecting her to challenge him. "Ever'body else's done gone home."

Verna sighed, wanting only to go home herself, but said, "Sure. Got any fresh coffee made?"

They waited, Verna on the sofa in the break room, Gary in his office. It was late, nearly six am. She was bone-weary tired. The room was cozy and warm, and she was dressed in many layers. She dozed. Verna startled awake when Gary touched her shoulder. "He ain't back." He looked at her deeply. "Ya gotta go 'n find 'im. He could be piled up some'eres. His papers gotta get delivered." For the first time since she'd met him, Gary Lawson looked almost apologetic.

Verna sighed. "Sure, Gary. On my way." She refilled her thermos, took the backup Laurelhurst run clipboard, and slogged into the storm again. She found Robert near the end of his route. Or, rather she found his van. As she made a turn, she saw two vehicles piled up at the base of a light pole at the bottom of a hill, fat, heavy snowflakes spinning in the wind, spiraling down in the cone of light illuminating the twisted metal like a strobe light on a modern art exhibit. Twisted around the light pole was a compact car; pinned next to it was Robert Graves' blue van. She shifted into neutral to coast and brake-tap to a safe stop, craning her neck to see if he was still at the wheel. Her chained tires, packed with frozen snow, lost traction and the van slid sideways. She could do nothing but try and steer. Her van slid into Robert's with a metallic screech and sickening bang.

As she sat considering what to do next, headlights appeared at the top of the hill to her left. Silhouetted in the swirling snowflakes from the hilltop pole lamp's cone of light was a big cab-over camper truck, paused for the moment. *Don't try it...don't try it...no no no...don't try it...you'll never make it down the hill!...* Unbelievably, the driver started down the hill, straight toward Verna. His tires lost traction; his top-heavy truck gathered speed as it skidded straight for her, its headlights growing bigger every second, slammed into her driver's door, spun around, and came to rest against the van's left side with its front facing the rear of the van. She wiggled out of her seat just before impact. No engine console between the driver's seat and the passenger's allowed her to squeeze onto the floor between them. The camper's collision caved in the van's driver's door and front left side. As she felt it shift under her, absorbing the tremendous impact, she grabbed her purse and her thermos from the passenger seat and crawled for the rear doors – the sliding side door and passenger door now pinned against Robert's van.

Outside in the vortex of swirling snowflakes and chilling wind, Verna batted snow from her eyes and surveyed the damage to the only vehicle she had ever bought new. Her stomach fell as she saw its twisted, mangled, sad state. The white cab-over and the black van, squashed together on their left sides, each facing the other's rear, both with headlights still on illuminating a shaken snow globe of a scene, looked like a crumpled Pisces icon or a Yin-Yang symbol pried apart. Verna was devastated as she looked upon her wrinkled, broken vehicle scrunched between a white truck and a blue van. It looked pitiful, as if it were trying to struggle free, its life's breath blowing steam out of its tailpipe because she had not had time to turn off the engine before the cab-over slammed into it.

Had she been able to hear her future-self attempting to bridge The River of Time, she would have heard that someday she would travel the nation in that very van as she and the love-of-her-life performed extraordinary shows that touched, and, yes, healed, the hearts of hundreds. But she could not hear that yet, for its revelation was not thus to come, and the whirling winds blew the undelivered message back across to dimensions yet-to-be.

The cab-over driver clambered out of his passenger side door, his driver's side pinned against her van. He was tall and thin, wearing a felted black cowboy hat, a light denim jacket, jeans, and sneakers without socks. Together they stood and looked at the pile of wrecked vehicles, then looked bleakly at each other.

"Sorry 'bout that, ma'am. I thought I could make 'at hill, okay. Guess I'se wrong, huh? You hurt?" Verna shook her head, mute, tears threatening. He chuckled ruefully, buttoned his jacket, and nodded toward the nearest house. "Looks like 'em folks're home. I guess we oughtta go call a tow truck, ya reckon?" He gestured toward the house below them, lamp lights casting golden rectangles on the fresh white snow.

Verna, seeing his bare ankles, said, "Just a second." She opened her rear doors and rummaged inside her emergency cardboard box. "Here. Put these on. Wool socks. Your feet must be freezing."

"Thanks." He stood a moment and removed his felt hat and placed it on her head over her wool cap. "There. That'll he'p keep tha snow outta your eyes."

Two survivors helping each other.

They knocked on the door which opened to reveal a cozy living room with a roaring fire in the fireplace, people, including Robert, sitting in easy chairs, dining room chairs, and on the sofa, all nursing coffee. The wonderful cinnamony, mouth-watering aroma of apple pie wafted into their cold noses. A small boy, wearing only his pajama top greeted them. "Hi! We got pie! Want some?" Two women welcomed Verna and the cowboy with plates of hot apple pie, and gestured to two empty stools at the kitchen's breakfast bar near the burbling coffee pot.

...Well...I felt something big rushing like a wind...had no idea it would be a wrecked van...good pie, though...Thank you, Heavenly Father, for sparing me from injury...

Verna asked to use the phone, called the warehouse, and reported the situation to Gary.

By the time tow trucks started arriving it was full daylight, gray though it was with swirling snow still falling. Fortunately, they brought containers of gasoline with them since vehicles of many stranded drivers had run dry, as Verna's van had with its last puffs of steam.

While sitting in the warm living room eating pie and drinking coffee, Verna and the others heard crunches of several other vehicles as they crashed into each other in the same place. All the drivers came in to use the phone. A total of ten vehicles piled up, only the light pole prevented the massive wreckage from sliding into their benefactors' yard. The compact car bent around the light pole was first; Robert's blue van was second in the pile, Verna's black van was third, and the white cab-over was fourth. The others were stacked together in so many odd angles, the mass of mangled vehicles looked like a Picasso painting or an Auguste Rodin abstract sculpture.

Once a tow truck driver freed Robert's van, he transferred his remaining bundles to Verna's, and they crawled up to the cab from the rear doors. Her van, though crushed in on both sides, was somehow drivable, rear doors functional. "Robert, why didn't you call the warehouse when you wrecked?"

"Well, I jus' figgered some'un 'ud come on out lookin' fer me. You know, like they's suppos'd ta."

"Yeah, well, you really caused a lot of grief and bother by not calling, y'know? All this could've been taken care of a long time ago when you first wrecked if only you'd've called."

"Yeah, I guess. 'At was good pie, though, weren't it?"

"Yes, Robert, I guess it was. But call next time, ok?"

"Yeah."

Slowly, they wobbled to the two remaining houses on the Laurelhurst run, spotted the papers, and shakily returned to the warehouse. On that long, slow return ride, Robert said only, "Thanks." Verna was too numb and tired to do anything but drive the crippled, bobbling van. *...It drives like a drunk dachshund...*

Gary Lawson was still where she'd left him, looking more bleary eyed than usual. Ned Flatt sat across from Gary's desk. Robert Graves shivered visibly, wearing only a lightweight jacket, jeans, and sneakers which were wet. He was bluish around the lips.

Verna reported all spots completed, both vans probably totaled, but she and Robert were uninjured. Insurance was discussed, and Mr. Flatt reminded them it was their responsibility to rent vehicles in which to report to work on Monday. They nodded, wanting only to leave so they could get some sleep. Verna, in silence, drove Robert to his house; then she nursed her damaged van – tire chains rattling like Marley's Ghost's, tires wobbling like a drunken sailor, van swaying as if it were a camel she was riding – to her warm, cozy manufactured home. She barely stayed awake long enough to peel off all her layers before falling into bed and asleep.

The black van was assessed to be within two hundred dollars of being totaled, so, instead of replacement, the insurance company paid for extensive repairs. While repairs were underway, Verna rented a van. It was of much lighter weight, much older, painted a hideous shade of yellow, and had no sound system or radio. Verna took her little tape player with her, set it on the passenger seat, and listened to her demo tape as she drove. Hearing her songs was reassuring. The rental van's heater didn't work, so the songs helped warm her.

In spite of this stormy beginning to 1987, with her precious van so terribly damaged, Verna retained that mysterious feeling of something flowing inside like a strong wind, carrying her along to…to *something*…something *big!* Whatever its source, it was within her, and completely independent of outer circumstances.

She continued writing songs, playing her guitar, and gradually became accustomed to sleeping in a still, quiet, Tasha-less bed. The little cat had occupied more space than one might expect, especially in Verna's heart. She gave all of Tasha's supplies to the Humane Society; she didn't linger there lest she fall in love with another cuddly feline. Verna made a firm commitment to not allow herself to fall in love again with any furry creature. The heartbreak at their passing would be an insurmountable grief.

Finally, repairs to her black van completed, she was once more behind its wheel. It was never the same, though. Just like a person who's been seriously injured, wounds can be surgically repaired, healing can happen, but it's not the same. She never again saw the cowboy who hit her, and Robert Graves behaved like a man deeply embarrassed because he'd been not only rescued by a woman but also scolded by one. He barely spoke and mostly avoided her thereafter.

As a "thank you" for their hospitality the night of the big storm, she baked cookies, chocolate chip and oatmeal cinnamon, for the two women at the foot of the hill who so generously welcomed all the drivers of the wrecked vehicles. Though quite startled at the gesture, they graciously accepted her thanks.

It was Valentine's Day. Big red hearts everywhere. Verna decorated the Lake City Distribution Center breakroom windows, and brought cinnamon sugar cookies dusted with red sugar sprinkles. She also brought Starbucks Viennese Cinnamon coffee to liven up the breakroom coffeepot. It was a festive day. That morning she'd written a new song entitled "Mama's Letters," a country ballad; she sang it silently under her breath as she always did when a new song birthed itself. So focused was she on her new song, she barely paid attention when Ned Flatt came to the warehouse that afternoon. The big man stood in the breakroom silhouetted against the heart-decorated windows, with a bleak expression on his otherwise friendly face.

"All of you here do good work." He nodded. "Good work." He paused, weighing his words. "There's going to be a layoff." Faces fell amid groans. "It has nothing to do with any of you *personally*. It's just a general layoff necessary to cut some costs here at The Times." He swallowed hard and took a piece of paper from his tweed jacket pocket. "Here's the citywide list of names. Everyone on this list will get a layoff bonus to help tide them over until unemployment kicks in." He moved to the bulletin board and tacked it up. "I'm sorry, everybody. This was not *my* decision." He did not look at Verna. His big red Cadillac sedan pulled smoothly away from the building.

Verna's name was on the list.

Navigating her way through the maze at the unemployment office was terribly difficult for Verna. She was in such shocked disbelief at being laid off, she could not retain information given her. An armload of paperwork still sat, untouched, on the kitchen table. She tried to play Michelle, but her stunned fingers weren't strong enough to fret chords. She read her dream journal, but none of it made sense. In some dim, still functional corner of her mind, she realized she needed to see Doctor Hale before her health insurance was canceled, so she made an appointment.

"Yeah. Laid off. Can you imagine?" Verna sighed and reached for her third piece of candy in that session. For the past year, she followed the Weight Watcher's program with Joe and Jean Couch and successfully lost enough weight to return to her size sixteen clothes. A small victory. Now, that didn't seem to matter. The pastel foil-wrapped chocolates were just what she wanted. Having gone so long without eating candy, its flavorful stimulation was all the more welcome.

Doctor Hale sat behind his big desk. Verna was his last patient of the day. He was saddened to hear her news, and even sadder to realize he was losing her as a patient.

"You need to realize that your occupation does not define you as a person. Your income does not define your worth. You, your guitar Michelle, and your songs are huge blessings to many. Your skill with a crochet hook has produced numerous warm gifts for many people." He gently touched the lacy white doily she'd crocheted for him – the one under the crystal candy dish – and smiled. "Right now is not a time to job hunt. Now is the time for introspection." He raised his grizzled eyebrows in query. "You can manage on unemployment for quite awhile, yes?" He gazed at her with his calm, gray eyes.

"Well, yeah. I suppose so. I mean my house payments are two hundred dollars a month, and the lot rent is one hundred dollars. Everything else is utilities and groceries. No pets to feed." Verna choked emotionally saying this but grabbed another piece of candy. "I do have the van payments to make and insurance, etc. Those are substantial." She swallowed the chocolate thoughtfully. "Maybe at last I can start sleeping like a normal person. I'll be glad to be free of this totally weird schedule. And Heaven knows I won't miss all the driving. I'm good at it, but I'm sure tired of it, y'know?" She shrugged. "I sure won't miss all the hard physical work either. My back hurts. My shoulders ache. My hands are callused." She peered at them. "And they're weathered. My hands look older than I am."

Doctor Hale smiled. "You'll have more time to play your guitar. Write more songs. You can nap whenever you want to. It would be a good idea to totally engage this period in your life. No need to run frantically around looking for another job. Just...*be*...for awhile. Its takes real talent to just...*be*." Doctor Hale smiled. "I'm sorry we can't see each other anymore. You, my dear, are a rare delight." His eyes twinkled.

Verna smiled in return. "Well, you are, hands down, THE best shrink ever, Doctor Hale. I'll miss seeing you once a month. I'll miss our sessions." The clock chimed, and Doctor Hale and Verna both rose.

"And this time, a hug for the doctor would be most welcome." He gently embraced Verna and said a silent blessing for her in his heart.

Verna filed for unemployment, and, while waiting for that first check, used her layoff bonus to clear all outstanding bills. With money left, she filled the gas tank, stocked the house with groceries, and took advantage of a yarn sale. She stopped by the guitar store to see the young man, Carl, who had become a friend she visited periodically.

"So, Carl, do you use a capo when you play? I've only just heard about them and I have one like this one." She gestured to one with the strip of elastic on it like hers.

"Well, not no more. I usta, though." He gazed at his guitar implements thoughtfully. "This'n is ach'ually better. It's a clamp, see? Look." He demonstrated how it worked on one of the shop guitars. "You can take it on an' off with one hand. Real easy. When you're not usin' it, jus' clamp it on tha end-a tha neck, like 'is. See?" He grinned at her over the guitar in his hands, now sporting a capo clamped to it.

"Huh. Well, would you look at that!" Verna smiled. "Carl, you have just simplified my life. Thanks! I'll take one."

She left the store with the capo in her pocket. Verna found it made it quite easy to change keys. When she got home, she sat with her binder of songs and went through them, experimenting with different keys. Even though it was mid-afternoon, she found herself nodding over the pages and lay down for a nap. She slept the clock around and awoke the next day.

Free of the arduous work schedule, Verna began to relax inside as well as outside. Doctor Hale was right. No need to start seeking work this instant. She could ponder awhile. She wondered what one could do with such freedom. She considered visiting her mother and her friends in Florida and Tucson, but then decided it best to spend money only on essentials. It also occurred to her she was now free to sign up for more classes and activities at the church. The next Sunday the senior minister found her setting up her Sunday School room, checking her supplies for the flannelboard story that day – David and Goliath. Always a favorite.

"Verna, our soloist called to say she has laryngitis. I wonder if you would mind leading the opening. You know, the call to worship, the "Our Father," and today's hymn. Oh, and our closing hymn, of course, "Let there be peace on earth."

Verna was stunned. "Well, certainly Reverend Furman, but who will take my Sunday School class? My kids?" Verna was uncertain. She felt honored to be asked, but she felt the kids would miss her.

"My daughter will take over for you, no problem." He smiled a sunny smile. "It's all settled then. You can lock your guitar in my office, and then please follow me to the sanctuary." Abruptly he turned and left. Verna followed, Michelle in hand.

In the minister's office she noted that it looked like any other executive office, a big desk, with orderly piles of papers on it, several mementoes here and there, photographs of his family. Large photos on the walls of groups of new members as they joined the church. *...Must be a great place to work...he's surrounded by all these smiles...* Verna tucked her guitar into the coat closet and they left, as he locked the office door behind him.

As they walked to the sanctuary, she told him she had been laid off a few weeks earlier, had more time than she used to, and was looking forward to joining two more evening classes. He stopped short and turned to her. "Laid off? You were fired?" He looked stricken.

"Well, yeah, sort of. Not fired because of bad performance, but because they're cutting back at The Times. Several other spotters were laid off as I was." Verna smiled reassuringly. "I'll be all right. I'm certain of it. I feel confident that God is closing that door because He's about to open another one."

"A better one," agreed the minister.

The service went well. Verna found she was not at all self-conscious about being on the stage in front of such a large crowd. She knew most of the people and was greeted by many smiling faces, which helped her confidence. Her strong voice never wavered.

March arrived in sweeping green splendor, verdant flora spreading across the city like a lush carpet, fully-greened deciduous trees standing amid tall evergreens punctuating the landscape like exclamation marks to spring's renaissance. Seattle was dubbed "The Emerald City" for a reason, and right now all it needed was a wizard to fully portray that magical place. More and more days were sunny, and people would say, "Look! The mountains are out." On such days, the Cascades shown in their icy grandeur, gleaming a dazzling bluish white in the spring sunshine. Mount Rainier reigned on the horizon like Seattle's own personal Olympus.

Verna began living life more like a normal person. She slept on a regular schedule. If she felt like doing something, she did it. If she felt like spending the day in her pajamas, she did that as well. There didn't seem to be any great sense of urgency about anything for the moment. She was at the church every day but Saturday, and loved every minute. She helped serve Wednesday night suppers and run the big dishwasher. She went out after church with friends for coffee and conversation, and found she enjoyed socializing with people. Reverend Furman's daughter was wonderful with her Sunshine Kids, so Verna was free to become part of the regular soloist rotation for the Sunday services and social gatherings afterwards.

"I've written some music and been invited to present it at another church this coming Sunday. Could you come and be there for me? I'm a little nervous." Verna's friend, Karen, indeed sounded a bit nervous on the phone. "I'm not like you. I get stage fright in front of people." She giggled self-consciously.

"Well, I get nervous, too, Karen. Feeling nervous just shows that you really care. When I look out over the sanctuary and see so many smiling faces, I forget for a while that I get nervous, and then, well, it's over." She smiled into the phone. "Of course I'll come. Now that I am not bound to that job, I'm living like a real person. I sleep at night, I do as I please during the day. I hadn't realized just how tired I was until these past few weeks of not having to go to work." She paused. "Of course I will one day go to work. I don't think unemployment checks last forever, right?"

Karen chuckled into the phone. "No. They do come to an end. You'll be all right, Verna. You're a strong woman. A survivor. No matter what happens, you'll be okay."

"Thanks, Karen. I'll see ya Sunday, okay? You'll be great." *...click...*

Dang!...I really hate to miss Sunday morning services at The Way!...But Karen's a good friend, and she'd go to something I'd ask her to go to...so, yeah,

I'll go support her…maybe some other friends from The Way'll go, too…that'd be nice…make it a special Sunday.

Verna could not have dreamed how special that Sunday would, in fact, be!

It was Sunday, March 27, 1987. Verna did indeed drive to the small church in Mountlake Terrace that morning to see her friend, Karen, present her original piano compositions for the Sunday morning service. Several other people from The Way came in support of Karen as well. After church they decided to go see the movie "The Mission" as a group. Then they went to The Great Pacific Dessert Company for some decadent chocolate mousse and discussion of the film. Afterward, her friend, Mark, drove Verna back to the small church where she'd left her van. She meant to drive north on I-5 to go home. Instead, she took the southbound freeway entrance and found herself headed toward downtown Seattle. She used to fume at herself for such mistakes. Now she just chuckled and muttered, "Guess I'm going to The Way after all. It's nearly time for Vespers."

Sometimes seemingly "instant miracles" prepare themselves for their advent long in advance of their arrival, readying themselves for their "season and time for their purpose under the heaven." Such a life-changing event was waiting for Verna as she drove toward it. Now was its time to be born.

That Sunday afternoon Norman Levine sat quietly on a bench in a Seattle city park across the street from the big church. In the fall of 1985, Norman, a former college theatre professor, and his wife moved from Nashville to Port Townsend, a Victorian seaport town on Washington State's Quimper Peninsula. He and his wife, in a last-ditch effort to "start over" and save their long-failed marriage, answered a nation-wide ad as winter co-innkeepers for The Olympic Inn, a Victorian bed and breakfast, while its owner took a winter-long vacation. Amazingly, from all applicants, they were accepted.

It was to be the "fresh start" Norman and his wife hoped would salvage their sinking matrimonial ship. It wasn't. It didn't work. They had not yet learned that changes in *location* do not change *them* because *wherever* they go, there *they* still are. Norman, his wife, and their failed marriage were merely in a different place.

During the Christmas Season of 1985, Norman, as co-innkeeper of the B&B, met Clarice Keegan, a freelance writer, artist, and photographer from Seattle. Tall, thin, with dishwater-blonde shoulder length hair cut in the style of Mick Jagger's, a pale Seattle complexion, strong jaw, merry blue eyes, always dressed in light gray sweaters and slacks with a red scarf around her neck, and wearing round "hippie-type" glasses on a brown beaded chain, Clarice was the epitome of a *creative artiste*. Her explosive, booming laugh filled a room, and she laughed often. Clarice, a "clarified soul amongst a comatose crowd," saw the hilarious absurdity within the human condition, and she often painted it, photographed it, or wrote about it. At the time Norman met her, she was writing an article on Washington State Victorian bed and breakfasts for a travel magazine, and she chose The Olympic Inn as her "headquarters" from which to write. She and Norman became fast friends.

In the summer of 1986 Norman and his wife separated, and in October his divorce finalized. He moved to Seattle where Clarice "took him in" and rented her spare room to him. In Seattle he "started over" with *his* new, single life. He became a member of The Way, located close by the Space Needle and a large downtown city park, the same park in which he sat on March 27, 1987. Norman liked that park with its dogwood trees, myriad blooming bushes, walking trails, and secluded sitting spots. Since he often attended The Way's services, he often "sat in the silence" in the park.

He was now in a position to fulfill a years-long dream. A professional story-teller and character actor, he had an idea for tandem storytelling with a partner. While living in Nashville, Norman worked in the Children's Section of the Nashville Public Library's main branch. He had the great good fortune to be apprenticed to a renowned Master Puppeteer, *a "Marionnettiste Celebre" as the French say,* Tom Tichenor. White-haired, soft-spoken, gentle Tom, the precise personification of Geppeto, famously presented marionette and hand puppet shows for children's groups in the downtown Nashville library's auditorium. As well as a marionettist, Norman also served as "straight man" to Tom's hand puppets as Tom worked them while seated within an enclosed puppet "theatre." Norman, performing as partner to a puppet, stood beside the puppet house and interacted with Tom's alternate personality, the puppet he used at any given time. Norman devised a technique in which two performers would switch places behind a puppet screen during a presentation while one performer worked a puppet as a character within a story. The other actor in front of the screen would interact with the puppet as the story unfolded. Depending upon the storyline, the two actors might exchange places behind the screen several times within a story as different characters. It was a unique and highly effective idea, a style that enchanted thousands.

Only it had not worked with his ex-wife who performed with him in Nashville while they lived there. Actually, their presentation process functioned very well; their marriage didn't. When they parted in Port Townsend, all he'd taken from their shared home were his clothes, his toiletries, and his storytelling puppets, props, and supplies. Norman yearned to follow his dream of entertaining, and he desired a female entertainment partner. He also craved a loving marriage; he sought a soul mate, as it were, for he understood that he and she would travel the nation as they presented their shows. So how could he find this partner of his? Pin announcements on laundromat bulletin boards? Take out ads in a newspaper? Stand on street corners and hand out flyers? No, he decided the only way he could ever find such a woman would be for God Himself to send her to him. Therefore, he commenced a twice-daily routine of intense, focused prayer. He "gave it to God" and trusted God would send her.

Thus he sat in the park in his solitude. He sighed in contentment, enjoying the gentle breeze and the rustle of the soon-to-bloom flowers all around him, bursting with life. No one bothered him. City noise faded away as he allowed his breathing to slow and went deeper into his inner silence. He pictured his perfect partner in his mind's eye – free to travel, free of child rearing, having a talent for the stage, willing to join him in his enterprise. He purposely did not picture her appearance or her type. He left those details entirely up to God. Deep in his heart he was absolutely certain God would send him the life partner for whom he prayed.

Norman usually attended morning services at The Way every Sunday. Today he had typically done so, but instead of catching the bus back to Clarice's house as he normally did after Sunday morning services, he decided he would catch the next bus at the bus stop across from the church and "ride its route" until it returned. He really didn't know *why* he decided to "sightsee," but it would be a good way to see parts of Seattle he'd never seen. And he could go to Vespers that evening before catching a bus back to Clarice's house.

Norman enjoyed the bus ride. Because it was Sunday afternoon, the bus was not crowded, and it was fun seeing Seattle as he never had, especially when the route climbed a hill overlooking the port with its orange cranes hovering like giant erector sets over docked cargo ships. The bus returned him to the park about 5:00pm. There was an hour in which he could pray before Vespers began. He slipped into the silence and began to feel a tremendous energy coming his way. It was unlike anything he'd ever felt or experienced before. It was filling him – *like a rushing wind* – enveloping him, saturating him, wrapping him in an energy cloak. It was indescribable, but palpable, profound, almost physical this energy was, close to overpowering, and it was coming toward him. He knew it was *her!* Somehow, with a knowing deep, deep inside – a knowing unlike any he'd ever known, a knowing that filled his every cell, a knowing so clear and complete there was not the tiniest minuscule of doubt – he *knew* the woman for whom he prayed was coming to the Vespers service, and they would meet that evening. *He _knew_ it!* With a confidence only God can give, Norman _knew_ it! Wrapped in that confidence, he walked into the church, sat close to the aisle on the third pew back from the front row on the right side of the sanctuary, and left a space beside him next to the aisle for her to sit. He had no idea *who* she was, how she looked, her age, her likes and dislikes – he knew *nothing* about her. He only knew she was sent by God, and that was enough to know.

Norman's and Verna's shared miracle was about to burst forth into its time and purpose. It had been long in preparation.

He sat and read the evening's program handed to him by an usher.

He felt her presence as she entered the sanctuary.

He felt her presence as she stood in the aisle by the pew on which he sat.

She entered the sanctuary at precisely 5:59pm and spotted a vacant aisle seat near the front, third pew back from the first row on the right side of the sanctuary. As she approached the man sitting there, his nose was buried in his program and she stood uncertainly, not wanting to interrupt. Just as she prepared to sit elsewhere, he looked up, smiled, and said, "I saved you a seat."

Verna sat next to him. She reached over, touched his hand, and said, "Thanks."

An electric tingle shot through her – *zapped through her, prickling every pore!* It was unlike anything she'd ever felt before. She looked again at the stranger. He had red hair, a full red beard, and the bluest eyes she'd ever seen. He was a leprechaun, a Viking, and a medieval king all rolled into one. She smiled. He smiled back and completely dazzled her. The Vespers service passed in a blur. All she could think about was this man next to her. While Verna did "go out" occasionally, it was always with a group of friends. Men sometimes made overtures, but she adroitly turned their attentions aside, not interested in getting into a relationship again...*ever* again! This man, however...well...*this* man...she'd never felt a reaction like that, so she kept looking at him askance. He caught her glance every time and smiled back. She felt herself blushing.

The service ended. They stood and talked in the aisle as people swirled and swarmed past them, headed for the exits. "Uh...would you like to go for coffee? Maybe somewhere we can talk?" Verna was astonished at herself. What in the world must he think of her for being so forward!

"Sure. That'd be great. Where would you like to go?" He smiled politely and waited.

"Uh...Denny's I guess. It's close by and they're open all around the clock. I used to stop by there sometimes when I had business downtown." Verna stood as if rooted. Finally she said, "My name's Verna. Verna Louise Hansen. What's yours?"

"Norman. Norman Levine. Very nice to meet you, Verna. Shall we go?"

Verna and Norman went in Verna's van to Denny's, ordered coffee, and sat and talked for hours. They couldn't take their eyes off each other. For both, though they only physically met, their "coming together" deeply felt like a reunion, a restoration of a relationship parted long ago, a renewal of an ancient heart-bond that was never broken. It was as if, somehow, their spirits knew each other, had searched for each other from a distant past, and had finally found one another again. It was indescribable, this feeling. Norman reached for Verna's hand.

"Is something happening here?" he asked.

"Yes, I think it is."

Finally realizing just how late it was, she said, "Well, gosh, this is really nice. But I guess we better go. Here's my card." Recently Verna, in a flash of intuition, had business cards printed that read simply, "Verna Hansen. LoveShine Inc." Only her phone number printed under the name. She'd supposed she might use them if somehow presenting her music to a producer someday.

They got in her black van and both leaned toward each other to fasten their seatbelts. As they did, spontaneously they kissed – a long, deep, soul-connecting kiss. That, normally, would have shocked each of them, for neither had *ever* kissed a person upon first meeting – *ever*! Yet it felt so natural, so normal, so *right*. For Verna, that kiss had a visceral impact. It was as if the entire universe settled itself into its proper order with an almost audible, *whump*. It was like the framed photos of her life on her inner walls suddenly set themselves level, and she never even knew they were crooked. Dizzy, she looked at Norman's blue eyes and red beard, and thought to herself, *"What manner of man is this?"* In a daze, she started the van and drove him to Clarice's house. He opened the passenger door to exit the van and smiled at her in the dome light's soft glow. "Do you go to the Wednesday evening supper?"

Wordless, Verna nodded.

"Guess I'll see you then. Good night." *It's too early to tell her she's the one I've prayed for. It's too early to tell her I knew she was coming to Vespers tonight. It's too early to tell her about the storytelling we'll do. I must wait for the right time. The right time will come.*

He closed the van's door and an engulfing inky blackness extinguished the golden glow. Norman disappeared into the night. He opened the front door of Clarice's house and walked in. She was sitting at her computer on the dining room table as she worked on an article for her monthly newsletter which was distributed to Seattle businesses. She looked up as he entered.

"Well, hello, stranger. I haven't seen you all day. You must've left early to go to church this morning."

"Yeah, I did. You're up late."

"Well, I've got to finish my newsletter. Got a deadline, you know. What've you been doing all day?"

"Oh, I decided to take a bus ride around Seattle after morning services. See parts of the city I hadn't seen. Then I thought I'd go to Vesper services. But you'll never guess what happened!"

"What?"

"Well, you know, I don't know how to describe it." Norman scratched his head, as if doing so would help in explaining the wonder he'd experienced. "But I met her tonight! You know I've been praying for a woman to be my entertainment partner as well as my life partner. She came to Vesper services this evening, and we went out to Denny's and just talked. It's her, Clarice! I met her tonight!"

"You what?"

"Yes! I did! Her name's Verna. I met her tonight! I don't know how to explain it, but I'll try."

Norman did his best to explain the tremendous energy he felt coming his way while he sat in the city park. He described how he knew "she" was coming to church that evening and how he left a space beside him on the pew for her to sit. He told Clarice about his conversation with Verna at Denny's and how they somehow kissed as they fastened their seat belts in the van.

"Well…wow, Norman. I'm happy for you. But be careful. Slow down."

"I know. I know. But what makes this different is that I've been intensely praying for the right partner, and you know I have really been doing deep inner work."

"Well…yes…I know you have. I understand that." Clarice was more logical than illogical, more "down-to-earth" than "flighty-woo-woo," more reasoned than unreasonable; yet she daily meditated and understood the Mind-Cosmos Connection. Although her "reasonable mind" somewhat doubted, her "meditative mind" – her "Zen core" – recognized realness. "Yes, I understand what you're saying, Norman."

"I've never done such concentrated prayer work before. Verna lives about a thirty-minute drive on I-5 north of here. I think I'll call her after she's had time to get home. I'll be quiet."

"OK. I'll finish this newsletter in the morning. I'm going on to bed. I'm really happy for you, Norman. I can't wait to meet her. I hope she's the right one for you."

"So do I. But after today's experience, she must be. From my prayer work and what happened to both of us today, she *has* to be. She *is*!"

The instant Norman closed the van door and melted into the night, Verna felt bereft. She'd never met the man before, yet she felt she knew him. Somehow, she felt in her heart they had always belonged together, and had just…somehow…lost each other along life's way. A stranger she'd never met, yet he also felt like a man she'd known for a lifetime. Perhaps many lifetimes. Her vision cleared, and she drove toward I-5, this time paying close attention to the freeway signs, driving mindfully as Doctor Dodd admonished her so long ago. She took the Northbound ramp and headed home. As she pulled into her carport, her phone was ringing.

She and Norman talked the night through as they "caught each other up" on their life stories and discovered their commonalities. Their conversation was more like two old acquaintances rather than people meeting for the first time.

"Norman, I don't know how it's possible, but I feel as if I've known you… well…all my life, sort of. Yet, I didn't see you until Vespers at six pm today." She sighed. "How could this be?"

"Well, however it be, it most certainly is," chuckled Norman. "It's one of His mysterious ways, I believe. Have you ever married?"

Verna told him about her husbands and unpleasant divorces. Then told him about her daughters. For some reason, she didn't mention her Chrissy. He was candid telling her his own history, including divorces and recent past. They chatted about many things.

"Tell me about your business card. What is LoveShine Inc.?"

"Oh. Well, I've written some songs, and a man I knew from The Times made a demo tape for me in his recording studio. I thought if I ever follow my mother's advice and shop the tape to music producers, it would be important to have business cards." She paused, considering what to say next. "I just want to make sure that I let the love in my heart shine through everything I do, whether it's sing, play, or...or...whatever it is. So I decided I would be, "LoveShine Inc." She waited, hoping he wouldn't think her foolish.

"Wow," he said softly. "That is amazing." He paused a moment. "You... write songs?"

"Well, yes, I do. But most of the time the songs just come, and I have to scramble to capture them. So to speak. Other times, though, I might see something and it will trigger a song that I write and figure out. That happened in the grocery store recently. Wrote the lyrics on napkins in the snack area." She chuckled a little. "I bought a guitar so I could learn songs. Never dreamed I'd be singing my own."

"I think that is just wonderful."

"Wow, Norman! We've talked the entire night. Do you go to work today?"

"Uh-huh. I work downtown at one of the banks. Temp job. Gotta catch the seven-thirty bus."

"Well, I'll say good night then. Or should I say good morning?" Verna giggled and caught herself. *Stop acting like a teenager...* "I'll see you Wednesday?"

"Oh, yes, indeed. I really look forward to seeing you again, Verna. I will talk to you again soon."

As they cradled their phones, the rising sun began to paint contrail clouds in streaks of pink as dawn's gray skies slowly bleached into blue.

A new day – a new life – was breaking for them both.

YES, IT'S REAL

...click...

Verna hung up the receiver, hating to disconnect from her hours-long conversation with Norman, but ecstatic from speaking with him – *more* than mere speaking; she opened her heart to him. She lay back on her pillow, holding the phone to her chest. She looked at her old Roy Rogers lamp on her bedside table. The old lamp was new when she was a small child. It had stood on every bedside table beside every bed she ever had, lit many a bedside youthful prayer, illumined countless pages of bedtime storybooks; it was an old friend. Throughout the years she had told Roy many of her dreams, childhood ones, broken ones, and those for which she yearned. As she lay there, breathing quietly, she said, "Roy? Do you know what's happened?" The cowboy just kept holding his hat aloft, grinning his ceramic grin, big golden palomino frozen in mid-rear, front legs forever pawing the air. Roy was like that. Whatever she told him, he just kept smiling and waving his hat – even when his bulb burnt out. He was very good at keeping secrets.

Verna's eyes heavily, and happily, closed. She slept.

Verna didn't sleep long. As she awoke, a song was nudging the edge of her mind. Having learned to pay attention to those, she arose and reached for Michelle. She sat on the edge of her bed, strummed a chord, and the entire song bubbled from her inner spring from which music seemed to just flow. The last line echoed in her small bedroom: "Come on let's fly this universe...for together we are...our wings..."

She opened her spiral bound song notebook and wrote the lyrics, complete with chords. There it was. In ink on paper. Definitely a ballad. A *romantic* ballad. *...Wow...what in the world is happening here?...he feels like he's...my...husband somehow...he's just in the wrong place...he belongs here with me...* Verna titled the song "We Are Our Wings."

She spent the day singing the song as she cleaned the house. In one of her classes at The Way recently, the facilitator used the example of the Widow's Oil from the Old Testament. She could hear his voice as she worked.

"God has blessings for everybody. You need to be open to Him. Remember the widow who was so sad? Through the prophet she was told to gather all of her jars, borrow her neighbors' jars, and get ready to expect a miracle. All she had in the house was a little oil and a little meal. She thought she would cook that and then she and her sons would just lie down and die. But when she opened her heart to God's possibilities, the prophet took the little container of oil she had and started filling the jars. He filled every jar she had. He filled every jar she could borrow. Only when her empty jars were all brim full, did the oil stop flowing." He grinned a big toothy grin and addressed the group. "So open your heart! God's gonna pour blessings down on you, and you need to get ready! You gotta make room for all the blessings that are coming your way."

Verna's bedroom had two closets. She emptied one and prepared bags to take to the donation store. She cleared out two drawers in her chest of drawers, and emptied the small drawer in the other nightstand.

...There...making room...for whatever blessings are coming my way...plenty of room now for lots of blessings...and for Norman's underwear...Verna! You're getting ahead of yourself, girl!

"So, tell me about being a professional storyteller." Verna sipped tea, as she sat at her kitchen table, talking with Norman on the phone.

He told her about being a professional actor and how he once traveled the country telling sea stories as he promoted a national seafood restaurant. He went to schools, performed one-man shows at school assemblies, and participated in parades as a sea captain.

"Are you Irish? My family's roots are in Ireland and Scotland, and we've got some storytellers for sure," Verna said with a chuckle. "My grandmother made me feel like I was right there with them in the covered wagon when they crossed the prairie and saw the great buffalo herds that made the ground shake when they ran."

"I think pretty much everybody has Scots-Irish roots" said Norman. "My family's roots are in England, I know for sure, and probably all over the UK." He sighed. "I would love to hear your songs."

Verna giggled. "I would love for you to hear them, too. Maybe you could come over Wednesday night after the service? I'm on the rotation to serve the light supper and run the dishwasher afterward. The guest speaker Wednesday night has a book out that I've been reading, so I really want to hear her speak."

"I'd love to come over Wednesday night," said Norman, the smile in his voice broader than ever.

"Well, it's on, then," said Verna. "See you Wednesday."
...click...

"And, Janice, he has a beard. A really full beard." Verna paused in her phone conversation. "Yes. Red hair and red beard. And Janice, he has the bluest eyes I've ever seen!" Verna sighed so that she nearly swooned.

"So, you've met a bearded Paul Newman, then?" Janice chuckled into the phone. It was great to hear Verna sound so happy.

"Who? Oh. Paul Newman, the actor. Well, actually, Norman is...well...much more handsome. Much more interesting. In fact, he's a professional storyteller and a character actor. He's...well...he's just amazing!" Verna sighed and looked out her window at the pond across from her living room. The ducks swam placidly, moving jerkily now and then whenever a catfish nibbled their webbed feet. There were some azalea blossoms open, so small blazes of hot and pale pink appeared here and there in the shrubbery around the pond.

"So, you've met a man more handsome, more interesting than Paul Newman? Wow, Verna. You've hit the masculine jackpot! How did you get so lucky?" Janice smiled across the kitchen at Derek who was listening to the one-sided conversation. She covered the mouthpiece for a moment and whispered, "She's good. She's better than good. She's...happy!"

"Well, I got lucky because I took a wrong turn. You know me, I've always had this right and left thing going on. It's a kind of...directional dyslexia...sort of. Anyway, I meant to go right and get on I-5 and go north to where I live. But instead I went left and got on I-5 going south toward downtown Seattle. And you know the funny thing? Once I got on the freeway, I didn't see any exits until I got to the exit for the church. It was kinda like...I don't know...this'll sound crazy, but it was kinda like the freeway sorta...uh...compressed itself... just kinda shrunk so the only exit I saw was the exit you take for church. So, I went ahead and went to the church and got there just as the Vespers service was to start. I went to the empty space next to him, and he told me he'd saved me a seat." Verna twirled her fingers in her hair – something she hadn't done since she was a teenager. "Looked up at me and said he'd saved me a seat...like he knew I was coming. Isn't that weird? Anyway, I sat down beside him and reached over and touched his hand and said 'thanks,' and, girl, I'm tellin' you, there was this... this...tingle that went all through me!"

"Static electricity?"

"No, Janice, not that. A different kind of electricity. Never felt anything like it before. Like my blood was buzzin'. Like the seat was electrified. Like a shiver, a shockwave all through me. Can't really explain it. I tell ya, this man is so... so...well...I just can't explain it." Verna realized she was tangling her hair so removed her hand.

"So, tell, girlfriend! What happened next?" Janice was smiling at the way Verna sounded.

"Well...we went to Denny's after church. Drank coffee. Talked. A lot. Then I took him home. But the strangest thing...we both leaned down to fasten our seatbelts and...we kissed."

"He kissed you! You went out for a coffee date, and...and he kissed you!" Janice sounded indignant.

Verna thought a moment. "No, not like that. It was more like...well...we kissed each other. We just sort of naturally met there, our heads touched, and... we just...kissed." Verna blushed at the memory. "I feel like I've always known him, and that I just now found him again."

"Oh. You knew him from somewhere before?" Janice was thoroughly puzzled now.

"No. Never met him until Sunday night. It's as if my heart knows him somehow." Verna sighed luxuriously. "Oh! And...I've written another new song. Wanna hear it?"

"Of course." She beckoned Derek to come to the receiver so he could hear, too.

"Okay. I'm laying the phone down and getting Michelle. Can you still hear me?" She heard tiny tinny voices saying that they could hear her. Verna strummed the opening chords and sang the first line.

"Today in my life there's music...by comparison, my life was still. Today in my life there's harmony sweet, where before was stubborn will..." On she sang until the last line of the last chorus. "Come on let's fly this universe...for together we are...our wings!" She picked up the receiver. "Well? Whaddya think?"

"I think it's your best. So far, anyway." Derek took the receiver from Janice. "Now listen, Verna, okay? Don't go gettin' all...ya know...head over heels silly, okay?" Derek took a deep breath. "'At's a beautiful song. Don' want ya ta waste it on some no 'count guy ya jus' met, y'hear? Jus'...slow down some...you don't know yet if this is even real. Heck-fire, ya don't know yet if *he's* even real. He got no car. He livin' with friends. Sounds like he don't have much in tha way-a prospects." Derek was pacing now. "You jus'...wal...you jus' go slow, girl. Hear me now? Jus' go slow. Don' wan'cha ta get all hurt er nothin'. Okay? Ya hear me?"

"Yes, Derek, I do hear you. But I've just never met anyone like him. He's just so...well...somehow I already know him. It's like I lost him for a long, long time and finally found him again. It's not like I'm meeting someone new; it's like I found someone I already know. It's like 'Where you been? Whatchu been doin'? I mean, we talked for hours on the phone the night I met him, an' it was like catchin' up with an ol' friend." Verna's fingers were twiddling her hair again. She pulled them away. "Anyway, I promise I'll be careful. Thanks, Derek. What did you think of the song?"

"Wal...like Janice said. It's yer best. I think it's real purty. Ya sure play 'at guitar fine. We gonna hang up now. Save ya a phone bill, okay? Take care o' yourself. An' 'member...slow down!"

...click...

GETTING TO KNOW YOU, GETTING TO KNOW ALL ABOUT YOU

1987 was a season of discoveries for both Verna and Norman. In a phone conversation she tried to explain their budding relationship to her friend, Karen, but found it wasn't easy.

"No, no it isn't like 'Love at First Sight' or some sort of infatuation. Karen, I'm telling you, it's like I've always known him and just...sort of...lost him for... for awhile." She paused. "Well, my whole life. But meeting him is not like meeting someone new. It's like rediscovering someone I've always known. Sort of...a reunion...kinda..."

"So...you love him, but...you just met him? That really sounds like what I understand to be 'Love at First Sight,' Verna." Karen sounded concerned.

"Well, to a lot of people, myself included, I guess it sounds like that. How can I explain that...that...electric tingle when I touched him for the first time? And... and...how do you explain the way we kissed each other in the van fastening our seatbelts? I've never, *ever*, in my life kissed a man the same night I met him. Or even on the first date! Yet, kissing him just felt natural. Lovely. Like the way happily married couples kiss each other. And, for me, it was like an internal alignment happened. Like everything in the world...the universe...was finally in its proper place." Verna sighed. "Karen, I think I've had my last first kiss." She chuckled a bit while suppressing a very teenage giggle.

"Will you listen to yourself? Verna, you are not the giddy type. I can't believe what I'm hearing. So who is he? Does he live around here?"

"He's divorced, staying with a friend. He's a professional storyteller and a character actor. He's coming to dinner tomorrow night. I can't wait!"

"Well, just don't lose your head over dessert, promise?"

"I promise. Gotta go. Love you, Girl. Bye."

"Bye, Girlfriend."

...click...

Karen laughed as she cradled the phone. She shook her head in puzzlement and, perhaps, a touch of jealousy. Twice she thought herself in love and was deceived both times. Karen lived inside her music and her career of writing computer code.

Norman in the passenger seat, Verna drove between the gate pillars of the manufactured home park and turned up the rise which led to her abode. Tastefully-placed colored lights in the shrubbery transformed the park into a twinkling fairyland at night. As usual, it was quiet, peaceful, and orderly. Verna had grown to love her home and was eager to show it to him. She coasted quietly to a stop in her carport.

"Well, here it is. My little refuge. For quite awhile I really resisted the idea of living in a trailer," she shrugged. "Well, a manufactured home. Bill Reilly, a realtor I know, recommended it, and he was right. It's perfect. Come on in."

Norman followed her up the porch steps and waited while she unlocked the door and turned on the lights.

"Verna, you have a lovely home here. You're right. It's perfect." He smiled and his blue eyes shone.

Verna melted. "Please let me take your jacket."

"Sure smells good. What is it?"

"Oh, I started a pot roast in the crock pot this morning. Should be just about ready. Don't you love it when you come home and dinner is already ready?" Verna smiled and set the table.

"Did you say you have a demo tape of your songs?" Norman stood in the living room looking at Verna's stereo. It was her one big indulgence. The other was her nice, warm, heated waterbed.

"Oh. Yes. It's in the player. I'm pretty sure I rewound it. Just press play." She busied herself with silverware and putting their dessert, an apple pie, in the oven to be ready when dinner was done.

"Little Girl Gone" floated from the speakers. Verna's voice, Michelle's honeyed guitar, and support instruments Gary Gerdes added blended in a warm, rich sound. There were three vocal tracks on which Verna harmonized with herself.

Norman stood transfixed, staring at the dancing green oscilloscope on the stereo as it oscillated with changing pitches.

"Well. What do you think?" asked Verna.

"Shhh..." Norman held up a hand. "I want to listen."

She came to him, took his hand, and gently led him to the table where supper awaited. Wordlessly, they sat, and tucked in to the simple homey meal of roast beef, onions, carrots, and potatoes. Verna baked bread earlier, and each plate had a slice of homemade bread next to it.

The bouncy, lively tune "Rainbows on the Ground" played next, and Norman looked up in surprise. He continued eating, but looked at Verna all the while. The timer on the oven sounded; Verna rose and set the apple pie on a trivet to cool. A cinnamony, apple aroma wafted through the little home. The air became moist with the essence of Christmas – soft, gentle, soothing – the sweet nostalgic perfume of timeless rightness, the pure scent of a happy home, its residents at complete contented ease at last.

Side One concluded, the tape stopped. "Would you like some more? There's plenty in the pot still." She smiled warmly at this man she only recently met but who felt to her like a husband who belonged precisely where he was. At her table. Eating his dinner.

"No, thank you." He smiled, removed his napkin from his lap, dabbed the corners of his mouth, and took a sip of sweet tea.

She plated the pie while Norman turned the tape over for Side Two. Silently, they enjoyed their dessert while listening together.

Verna's living room was furnished with two green upholstered rockers, between them a small table on which rested a lamp, and in front a small coffee table she had sanded and refinished. Opposite from her stereo was her television. Verna started coffee, and they settled themselves comfortably in the rockers.

"Please may I hear it again?" Norman smiled gently. "From the very beginning all the way through to the end?"

Verna rose and restarted the tape. She turned off the kitchen lights, and they sat in the lamp's soft glow. Easily they reached for each other and held hands. It felt perfectly natural. Verna had never been so completely at ease with a man. Everything about him seemed familiar. She just let the wonder wash over her. Her voice, her music, her guitar, filled the air. Norman, absolutely astounded, listened as the "feeling from the park" filled him once more.

Oh, Dear Lord, what a beautiful voice she has! What incredible talent! Oh, Dear God, thank You for answering my prayers. It is time now. It is time to tell her about my dream, about the entertaining we will do. It is time because I really know she is the one I've prayed for. Thank You, Father.

The tape stopped and they sat, replete, in the lamp's dim light. Outside, frogs croaked distantly in the pond, and the spring night gently enveloped them. Norman spoke into the softness, "Who *are* you?" Neither spoke. "I think it's time to show you who I am." Releasing her hand, he went to the van. She heard the door open and close with a thump. He'd left his briefcase by his seat. When he returned he gestured at the table, turned on the light, and they sat together.

"Singers have Demo Tapes. Actors have portfolios. This is mine." He opened a large binder on the table.

Verna turned page after page of photographs and newspaper articles of Norman Levine. There he was as a sea captain in several photos. She turned another page, and there he was as a Viking. On another page he was an old prospector. There was a newspaper clipping of his promotional appearances as a town greeter. There was a photo of a poster announcing a community event he'd produced. He'd acted in a movie. He'd directed plays. He'd written plays. He'd been a college Drama Professor. As she turned pages, he began to tell her his dream of a tandem storytelling act and how it could work. She learned he was also a puppeteer. Verna found him utterly enchanting.

"Wow! You are amazing!" Verna grinned at him in delight. "You've done all of this?"

"Yes, indeed. The proof is in the pictures." He stood and refilled their coffee cups.

She turned the next page and gasped. There was Norman. His hair and beard were not red but white, and he was dressed in white fur-trimmed red velvet as Santa Claus. Verna rocked back in her kitchen chair, and gasped. *"You* are Santa Claus?" Her jaw dropped, and her eyes rounded.

"Well, yes. I'm a character actor, and Santa is one of my characters. I bleach my hair and beard for Christmas. It's not naturally white yet," he chuckled.

Verna told him a story from her childhood, a conversation with a visitor who came to her parents' home in Germany when she was eight years old. The man, seated on the opposite end of the couch from where she sat, held a cigar. He turned to her and said, "So, tell me, little girl, who do you want to marry when you grow up?" He struck a match and lit the cigar. When she replied, she couldn't see his face at all – just a glowing fiery coal in the midst of a cloud of dense blue smoke.

It felt as if she spoke into Eternity.

"I'd like to marry Santa Claus when I grow up."

The man laughed, extinguished the match, and the cloud dissipated, revealing his face once more, the cigar once again only a cigar.

"Oh, really? And why would you want to marry Santa Claus?"

"Well...he likes animals because he has eight reindeer to look after, and Rudolph, of course, the one with the shiny nose. He likes to travel. He's very nice to everybody. He laughs a lot. He likes to give presents and he's jolly. He also likes my cookies because he ate them all last Christmas Eve. Yes. I want to marry Santa Claus when I grow up."

Verna sighed in recollection and at the miracle she was telling her story to a man who really *was* Santa Claus.

Norman sat at the table, stunned. He took a deep breath and let it out. "Well." He seemed at a loss for words. He breathed deeply once more.

"I've told you who I am, Verna, and I've told you of my dream. Now it's time to tell you why I saved you a seat at church Sunday night."

He told her of his intense prayers for his perfect partner. He told her how he'd felt her coming to church on the night she had accidentally gone south instead of north, of the tremendous energy coming his way. "I saved you a seat at the Vespers service because I *knew* you were coming. I honestly didn't know *who* was coming, but I *knew* the perfect partner for whom I prayed was coming. And it was *you!* God was sending you to me. Thank God, it was *you!* I haven't said any-thing about that before now because I didn't want you to think I was crazy. And I wanted to be absolutely certain before I told you. I was pretty sure the moment you sat down beside me in church, but listening to your tape tonight made me *absolutely* certain. God brought us together, Verna. This may sound insane, but I think He's brought us together *again!*" He smiled softly. "And now...here we are. I feel like I've known you forever." He reached across the table and took her hand.

"Me, too, Norman. Do you feel kinda...well...sorta married?" Verna blushed, but she held her gaze.

"As if we've always been," agreed Norman. They stood and kissed, a long lingering kiss. Without realizing she was doing it, Verna turned and was leading Norman down the hall to the bedroom. She caught herself and stopped midway.

"Norman." She took a deep shaky breath, placed her palm in the middle of his chest, and said, "I want to do this right. I've never been one of the...the 'fast girls'...as such girls were called when I was a teenager. Please don't think me forward, but I really, really want to make love to you." She stopped for a moment and then words rushed out. "But I want to do this right. Do you understand?"

He nodded his head, kissed her softly, and turned back toward the kitchen. "Yes. I want to do this right as well."

"Norman, I've written you a song. I'd really like to sing it for you if that's all right." Verna blushed, rose pink flooded her face. *Get hold of yourself...you're getting more teenager-ish by the minute...*

"Well, that would be lovely." Norman sat in his chair, hands comfortably clasped over his middle.

Verna removed Michelle from her case, placed the strap over her neck, stood in front of Norman, strummed the opening chords, took a deep breath, and sang.

"Today in my life there's music...by comparison my life was still. Today in my life there's harmony sweet...where before was stubborn will. There's compliance instead of rebellion...joy is beginning to sing...the door to love is opening...with you I'm finding my wings."

She sang the ballad to its conclusion, *"...Come on let's fly this universe...for together we are...our wings!"*

Norman sat, speechless. Spellbound. He spoke finally. "Wow. When did you write that?"

"The night we met," answered Verna softly, with love in her eyes.

They sat in the green rockers, held hands, and talked late into the night.

"Clarice, I want you to meet Verna Hansen. Verna, this is my friend, Clarice, the writer I told you about. She has been so gracious as to rent me her spare room. Clarice, Verna. Verna, Clarice."

She smiled warmly. "Come on in. I've just made some coffee cake."

They were in Clarice's house on a quiet street in Seattle. It was an old, three story house with enormous ancient trees around it. It was built back in the days of big yards, and the lush back yard was grand with green grass and ripe with red clusters of rhododendrons, purple azaleas, yellow spatterings of black-eyed susans, and dottings of dogwoods in special spots. The studious ambiance of a working writer as well as museum-quality paintings and photographs of a creative artist filled the house. It was a singular house in a singular city, "The City of Flowers," more famously known as "The Emerald City."

As Clarice dished up cake and poured coffee, an enormous black and white cat sauntered into the dining room, plumed tail aloft, and leapt into Verna's lap, peering closely at her face. It kneaded her lap with soft paws, purred, turned, and settled itself into a curled furry mass, contented.

"Well, you've just been cat approved," chuckled Clarice.

"I love cats. Two of my best friends have been cats. They can be real lifesavers." She petted the soft fur and rubbed the cat behind the ears, causing it to arch its neck in pleasure.

"So, you just met Norman, right? At church?" Clarice took a tiny bite of coffeecake and reached for her coffee cup.

"Yes. But I feel as if I've known him all my life." Verna smiled at Norman. "It feels more like I finally found someone I lost after a very long time of looking." She sipped her coffee. "Thank you for the cake. It's delicious." She smiled at her hostess.

"Tell me, Verna, what do you do?" Clarice stirred her coffee and pondered her closely.

"Well, right now I collect unemployment. I was recently laid off from the Seattle Times."

"Reporter?"

"No. I was a spotter. I delivered bundles of newspapers to carriers. That's why I drive a van. It's required for the job. I bought it new just last year, but it got damaged in a ten-car pileup in that unexpected blizzard we had."

"Really? Ten cars?"

"Yes. But I'm fine. The van is repaired. It still drives like a drunk dachshund sorta, but it's all fixed according to the insurance company." She smiled at Clarice a bit uncertainly, not sure what to think of this friend of Norman's.

"So, Clarice, as I was telling you, Verna and I plan to be married. We're going to get the license tomorrow. Won't you come and be a witness? It would mean a lot." Norman smiled and took Verna's hand.

Clarice's eyes went large and round. She laid down her fork and stood. "Excuse me." She rose and turned toward the kitchen.

Norman and Verna looked at each other. Norman shrugged. Clarice returned with the coffeepot to fill the cups, and sat.

"Wow. Married! Thanks. I'd be honored." She stirred her coffee releasing wisps of steam. She pondered a moment then looked up and said, "Isn't this a bit sudden, you two? I mean...well...you just met, right? Shouldn't you get to know each other a bit better before you launch yourselves into...into matrimony?" She looked from one face to the other and gulped.

Norman and Verna burst out laughing. Norman reached to touch her hand in reassurance. "It's all right, Clarice. We already feel as if we've known each other for a lifetime. We'll spend the rest of our lives learning about details, but basically we already feel married. We just want to do this right."

"It's true," said Verna. "A lifetime. Already."

Clarice sighed, glanced down at her hands a moment then looked up. "Well, all right then. I'll be a witness." She laughed and shook her head helplessly, held her cup aloft, and said, "A toast. To a lifetime of learning details!"
   ...clink...

LAUNCH

Over their lunch of cheese sandwiches with tomato and green onion salads, Verna looked fondly at Norman and said, "Thank you for not requiring me to change my name when we got married. It was already changed twice before, and, well, it just gets...complicated. You know?" She took a bite of her sandwich and suddenly felt a little embarrassed, though she couldn't say why.

"It must be hard for women. I mean when a boy is born, he is given his father's last name. When a girl is born she is, too. But then she marries and she has to change her name to her husband's last name. And if she divorces and remarries, then she has to change her last name again." Norman chewed and swallowed. "Verna...have you ever wanted to get your own name back? You know...your maiden name...your birth name…Davidson?"

Verna paused and thought. "Well, of course I have, but it seems so...I dunno... complicated. I'd have to go to court, I guess....and probably have to fill out a lot of paperwork, no doubt...and it just sounds kinda...like too much trouble."

Gently, Norman took her hand. "It's your name. You can choose what you'd like it to be. So why not take your name back? Your own identity?"

She looked up slowly. "I could, couldn't I? I could take my own name back. I could get...*me*...back. Verna Louise *Davidson*." Unexpected tears rose in her eyes. "Thank you, Norman. Thank you."

"What's this one called again?" Verna peered anxiously at Norman from behind the puppet screen. It was a magnificent, 3-dimensional, soft-sculptured fireplace, made like a quilt, supported by a PVC pipe framework. The red bricks, white mortar, yellow and red "flames," and brown mantelpiece looked very "homey" and inviting on a stage. Currently, it occupied a great deal of Verna's small living room.

"The Tailor." Norman smiled at his storytelling partner, his new wife. It had been a simple, yet momentously profound and meaningful, marriage ceremony held in Clarice's back yard among the azaleas and dogwoods so glorious in the Pacific Northwest. Clarice turned out to be more than a witness! She hosted the wedding! A proficient photographer, Clarice also recorded the occasion on film, providing precious photographs long cherished. Reverend Furman, senior minister of The Way, officiated the small ceremonial attended by a few well-wishers. Reed Evans and Karen, her friends from The Way, were there. Joe Couch, Verna's past supervisor at The Seattle Times, his wife, Jean, their son, CJ, and Paulie, Verna's former co-worker at The Times were there. So, of course, were Clarice and her daughter, Shanti, a beautiful young woman with long flowing brown hair. As a special feature of the ceremonial, Shanti blessed them with a Druid wedding prayer, *"We swear by peace and love to stand heart to heart and hand to hand. Hark, O Spirit, and hear us now confirming this, our sacred vow."* She then read from Kalil Gibran's writings on marriage.

"You were born together, and together you shall be forevermore. You shall be together when the white wings of death scatter your days. Ay, you shall be together even in the silent memory of God."

How true! Verna thought then. *Norman and I <u>were</u> born together. We were together in the white wings of death. We have always been together in the silent memory of God. That's why he was so familiar to me when we first met. That's why we knew each other from the minute we found each other again! That's what I tried to explain to Janice and Derek and Karen! Shanti understands! Bless her!*

"The Tailor," Norman continued, "doesn't require puppets. See? Everything gets mimed. Let's try it again." He gestured for her to come out around the fireplace and stand to his right, which, he explained, would be "stage left" to the audience.

They rehearsed the tale of the tailor who created himself a magnificent coat, and "he wore it and wore it and wore it until it was all...worn...out." Verna felt the presentation needed something...*more*...somehow. She didn't know quite what, and she was, in a very real sense, Norman's student. *But still...*

"That's it. You're getting it. You're doing very well, my love. How do you like it?" Norman grinned. *She's perfect...a natural...her sense of timing is impeccable.*

"Oh, I like it fine." Verna poured some sweet tea and took a big drink. The windows were open, and sunshine streamed in on this beautiful day. Storytelling was hard work, and she was thirsty. She set the glass down and stood, uncertain. "Uh...Norman? Do you think it needs, I dunno...something else...something more?"

"What? What does it feel like it needs?" Eyebrows raised, Norman waited. He'd dreamed he would actually find a partner as gifted as she, and he trusted her instincts.

"Well...something to kind of...keep the rhythm...the feeling...of the story going in between sections. It sort of falls flat somehow in the middles." She stood a moment. "I've got an idea. Let me try something." She hastened to Michelle's case, removed her, and quick ran through the strings to tune them. "Now. Let me try a little guitar introduction, like this." She strummed some chords, and nodded to Norman. "Do the intro...the 'Once Upon a Time' part..."

They started the story again, this time Verna playing chords under the lines as they unfolded, undergirding phrases like guitar-supported stanzas of a song. Sure enough, the guitar added another element to the story, another "voice."

"That's great, Verna! Excellent! Never in a million years would I have thought of that!"

"Well, movies have soundtracks. Sometimes it's a recognizable theme, but most of the time it's just musical sound that helps...add suspense, say...or maybe quickens the pace like in a cartoon. Or perhaps resolves in a resounding major chord to indicate a big finish. A musical Ta-Da! Like this!" She demonstrated, and they both laughed.

Norman hugged her. "You're right. Any time we can, we'll add Michelle's voice to the performance." He smiled into her eyes, flooding her with such love she nearly swooned.

They practiced daily. Norman taught Verna how to move on a stage, deliver lines, and move in tandem with a storytelling partner. To Verna it was all fun. What she enjoyed most, though, was being with Norman.

"What shall we call ourselves, do you think?" asked Norman one morning as they were waking up, soft streams of golden sunshine illuminating the small, cozy bedroom, glinting little gold sparks from his red hair. "Y'know, when I was a single storyteller, I called myself 'The Tellerman," like I told you once. Maybe we could be 'The Tellerman and The Tellermiss?' Or 'The Tellerman and The Tellerma'am?' That's kinda catchy."

"Oh, I don't know," yawned Verna as she snuggled into his shoulder. They slept in each other's arms, entwined like octopi. Neither could ever get close enough to the other. "Um...Mr. And Mrs. Storyteller perhaps?" She yawned again. "Y'know...in ancient times bards and storytellers could travel safely even in times of war, as they carried news from village to village. They would often make current events, or tales of a battle, into a rhyming song. They'd use a little harp, a penny-whistle, or small flute to play a short musical phrase between spoken sections. The bards and storytellers crafted history into something memorable. Heck, we even do it today. Civil War songs reinforced soldiers' loyalties and helped them understand why they were fighting." Verna yawned hugely again, hugged Norman, and turned on her side to roll out of bed. The waterbed sloshed, causing Norman to rise and fall on the small wavelet. "Sooo...songs definitely helped tell stories. Or maybe sing a story. A song that tells a story can get stuck in your head and then you always *remember* the story."

Norman lay there, rocking gently in the warm cushy waterbed, pondering. *Tell a song...sing a story...hmmmm...* He heard Verna singing the song she wrote for Susanna as she puttered in the small kitchen. "There's a rainbow in the sky, there's a rainbow on the ground...look, Mommy, rainbows all around..." She sang often. When they first met and she told him about her family, she explained that singing through the day was simply second nature. Her family traveled a lot, so they sang in the car, sometimes with the radio, old cowboy songs her dad knew, or hymns and ballads. The family sat on the porch of her childhood home and sang the sun down. Neighbors often gathered in the dusk to sing with them. She'd told him her dad used to say she was born singing. He smiled inwardly. Norman had come to believe it.

Verna was just stirring – in that murkiness between sound asleep and fully awake she heard music. Keeping her eyes closed, she focused and concentrated as she'd learned to do once songs started coming.

...A teller of songs and a singer of tales...a StorySinger am I...Come everyone and gather 'round...to Wonderland we shall fly...

Immediately she arose, leaving Norman asleep and breathing gently. She reached for Michelle, sat in a kitchen chair, and strummed. With a natural ease the chords came and fitted themselves to the lyrics. After playing it through a few times she waited quietly to see if there was more to the song. Nothing else came. She wrote what she had. *Hmmm...not much of a song...more of a...a...short theme song I think...this is it!...Our theme song...Our entertainment name!...*

"Norman! Norman, Sweetheart! Wake up. I've got our name. Come and hear." She played it through again. Norman, still sleepy and gilded by the early dawn light, came and sat in the other chair.

"What? What have you got?"

She played it for him. His eyes went wide and his eyebrows shot up. "You did that? Just now?"

Verna nodded, and smiled. "I woke up with it. We're going to be called 'The StorySingers,' and we'll open our shows with our theme song, like this." Verna sang the inviting little tune again.

Norman clapped his hands in delight. "You are a wonder! It's great! Short. Snappy. Says what we do. Better than 'The Tellerman and Tellerma'am!' 'The Tellerman' never sang a story!"

The rest of that morning over scrambled eggs and toast they tossed ideas around and by lunchtime had created an introduction to use in conjunction with the theme song. Verna taught Norman to sing. Although he begged off at first, claiming he hadn't sung since he was in Sunday School decades ago, she finally convinced him, and they sang their theme song together in harmony. They would always open their shows with their theme song. It became their trademark.

"Sew? Well, yes, I did learn to sew. Under duress!" laughed Verna in response to Norman's question. "I mean, heck, I can mend something using the sewing machine, and I've even been known to cut out a pattern and sew a dress or a blouse, but I don't consider myself real good at it. Why?"

Norman's blue eyes twinkled. "Well, because we're going to need costumes. Storytelling costumes." He kissed her.

"Show me what you mean. Can you maybe sketch it?" Verna waited, eyes troubled. She had indeed learned to sew way back in Junior High when the class project was a ruffled pinafore. It had not been a pleasant experience, and she hadn't touched her sewing machine in years. In fact, it was a small miracle she even still had it. Jerry brought it after she'd moved out, thinking it a reasonable enough errand to give him an excuse to try to talk her out of the divorce. It hadn't worked. The sewing machine sat on a closet shelf, unused, all this time. She wondered if it was even still functional.

She watched over Norman's shoulder as he made some rough sketches, and some concepts began to form. *Hmmm...long skirt for me...long sleeved shirt and long vest for him...maybe a storytelling coat that looks sort of old timey...Hmmm... patchwork maybe...a touch of crocheted lace...* Ideas perked like a percolating coffee pot, a few slow blurps-blurps at first, then blurping faster and faster until a complete, delicious pot of coffee steamed or an entire costume waited in her head to be manifested through her hands.

At a thrift store Verna bought several party dresses of fine fabric: satin, brocade, taffeta, even silk and velvet. Carefully she used her seam ripper to take them apart, ironing the fabric pieces flat and using them to create costumes of her own design. For a brief moment she remembered her ironing days and smiled softly. *...Verna Louise you've sure come a long way...* For Norman she made a gold paisley storytelling vest from a stylish coat she'd found. The tag read "raincoat," but she decided it was mislabeled. It was a gorgeous paisley print on a shiny gold background and went great with Norman's red hair and beard. She added a brown velvet collar, and matching pocket flaps.

Looks good if I do say so myself...

Day by day they worked on their presentation; timing grew closer and closer until they were seamless. They discovered they were very good together. Norman's temp job at the bank concluded and now they spent every day designing a show. Norman had several ideas in his notebook, and now, with Verna, could implement them. Together they adapted classic fairy tales into their own unique style and created original stories and songs. Verna captured and wrote songs as they came or would craft a specific song for a particular story. She amazed herself. The Seattle Times Spotter part of her was receding, now a fuzzy figure in the rearview mirror of her mind...the OR Nurse dimmer yet. This singing storyteller she was becoming was looming large on the windshield of her life, and she reveled in it. Her love for Norman was such that if he asked her to fly, she would probably figure out a way. They kept at it every day, Verna learning new stories, learning how to operate the Muppet-style puppets, or, in the case of "The Frog Prince," how to convincingly mime throwing and catching a golden ball. Staging, performing-in-tandem, interpreting, gesturing, all elements of polished, professional performing became easier and easier.

Determining the charge per performance was difficult, however. One afternoon Norman, occupied with tablet and pen, studied over the problem while Verna napped. There was a worry crease between his brows.

As she snoozed, Verna dreamed she was zipped up in the mummy sleeping bag she and Jerry used during their trip from Tucson. Feeling a need for the bathroom, her dreamself fumbled with dream fingers for the zipper. Instead of a zipper tab, she found a loose thread and pulled on it, opening the bag's neon orange nylon shell. Still fumbling for the zipper in her sleep, she dreamed she was pulling wads of fiberfill from the sleeping bag. Only it wasn't soft. It was crackly. Like folded paper. Her dream eyes opened, and she looked at what was in her hand. She saw very clearly a fifty dollar bill. As she raised up a bit, she saw wadded fifty dollar bills all over her chest and on the bed next to her. The sleeping bag was stuffed with money! Then she awoke in earnest, lying on top of the bedspread as when she laid down for her nap.

"Norman. Hey, Honey, I know what to charge now." She got up and went to her husband sitting at the table frowning over a tablet filled with figures.

"Huh? I'm sorry, what did you say?" He smiled, seeing her walk down the hall toward him, an aura of ideas radiating from her like moonglow.

She told him about her dream and the fifty dollar bills. "So, see, that's the answer to what to charge. No matter the engagement, no matter the setting, no matter who it's for, no matter the travel distance, we charge fifty dollars a performance. For now." She grinned and sat down.

Norman pondered a bit and glanced at his figures where he was trying to determine charges for mileage traveled, extensive set-up, performance with puppets and without. He marked a big X over the page and said, "By golly, you're right. Fifty dollar bills. Keep it simple. Get our name out there. You're a wonder!" Verna leaned over and kissed him. "You, my dear, are the wonder." She gazed into his eyes. Norman decided it was "nap time" for them both, took her hand, and led her down the hall back to the waterbed.

"Norman, how are we going to get out there?" She gestured vaguely out the door. "How are we going to find a place to perform? I think things are coming together really well, don't you? I feel like I'm ready to go do it!" She smiled at her partner. Her eyes sparkled with future potentialities. "How do we start finding a venue? When do we start?"

"We start now" He opened the phonebook's yellow pages to daycare centers. "We'll start here." He placed his finger at a name on the page and picked up the phone. For most of the day he dialed numbers and spoke to people. presenting the idea of them coming to tell stories and sing songs. Tom Nation, the Music Therapist who taught Verna basic chord patterns, had explained that if she used what he gave her, there wasn't any song she couldn't sing with the guitar. She believed it, so consequently taught herself several songs that could work in a group sing-along for just about any age. As a resource, she even had the Mesquite Valley Mental Health Hospital's songbook in its worn orange binder. With her capo, she could pitch any song in any key.

"Is this the right place? Are you sure?" Verna gazed out the passenger window of the black van at the small pink building decorated with dancing alphabet blocks. Norman glanced down at the scrap of paper in his hand and said, "Yes. This is the address. I'll go check in with the director, okay?" The door closed behind him with a solid thump. With a slight shudder Verna remembered the impact on that door when a white cab-over camper slammed into it the night of the blizzard. This was a new door, and it sounded like one.

Verna sat there, nervous in her recently hand-created finery, and felt a flutter of butterflies in her midsection. She was astonished to find herself nervous. *Not stage fright exactly...but definitely nerves...* She gave herself a stern talking-to. *What is the matter with you? These are just little kids. Like your Sunshine Kids. All little kids like stories. All little kids like to sing...*

Norman returned, smiling. "They're all ready for us. Get your guitar, and I'll get the fireplace and puppets." In addition to learning and practicing stories, Verna also practiced putting up the set. To her the activity felt familiar, somewhat like preparing an operating room prior to surgery. Props were arranged logically in the order in which they would be needed. *Huh! Just like setting up instruments in order on a Mayo Table...wow!...who knew when I handed a scalpel to a surgeon, I'd someday be handing a prop to my performing partner just the same way...amazing!*

It _was_ amazing, that very first performance! It was also a learning experience. The children were ushered "choo-choo style" into the playroom, each child's hands placed on the shoulders of the child in front. Once stopped, they immediately plopped down on their bottoms on the floor, eyes big and round looking expectantly at Verna, Norman, and the big fireplace. The director addressed the group. "Children, this is Mr. Norman and Miss Verna. They are here today to tell us a story. Let's all be nice and quiet so everybody can hear." She clapped her hands to lead the applause for their beginning.

For the first time, Norman and Verna introduced themselves to an audience. "This is Verna Louise Davidson," Norman indicated Verna to his right. "This is Norman Elias Levine," Verna responded, indicating Norman to her left. "And we are..." Norman said. "The StorySingers!" they said together. Then they sang, "A teller of songs, and a singer of tales. A StorySinger am I. Come everyone and gather 'round. To Wonderland we shall fly." It was their first introduction of hundreds to follow in the years yet to come.

With the magic words "Once Upon a Time" the show commenced. They performed three stories, ending with "The Tailor" and its new guitar accompaniment. They closed with the song "If You're Happy and You Know It" so the children could stand up, clap their hands, stomp their feet, and "choo-choo" back to their snack room.

Verna felt somewhat astonished at herself. They'd done it! They'd done their first show! The first of many, according to Norman. It was a success. The Daycare Center's Director enthused over their performance, and Norman asked if she would write a reference letter to be included in future mailings. She was happy to do so and wrote their check and provided the letter.

Set packed and back in the van, Norman and Verna looked at each other and burst out laughing.

"Well? What did you think?" Norman peered at her over his glasses.

Verna let out a whoosh of air, then took a deep breath. "I think that was...that was...fun!" She paused. "When can we do it again?"

"Just as soon as we get another booking." He put the van in gear and they high-fived each other. "We're off and running now, Honey. Who knows where this will go, but I think it's gonna be great!"

One Sunday at The Way a very special guest, Reverend Charles King, presented the service. He was an incredibly dynamic black man, an operatic baritone, who had toured the world singing in nearly every country, including South Africa during apartheid. In South Africa he was issued a special ID card with his photograph which identified him as white so he could freely travel and enter venues where he was booked, so valued was his talent. His interactive performances unified audiences across the globe.

The Sunday service was unlike any Verna or Norman had ever experienced. Reverend King got the congregation singing songs that he taught the group line-by-line. He had them hold hands and sing to each other. He taught them canons and rounds. He led them in joy songs. It was glorious! When the hour was up, the congregation wanted more. Many stayed for the next service. The entire experience was overwhelming in a very good way.

They met with him after the eleven o'clock service. He grinned broadly. "How do you do, Norman and Verna. Reverend Furman told me about you. You're The StorySingers. Right?" They nodded shyly. "I'd like to invite you for a visit. I live with my family in Yakima, just over the mountains. It's a big house. We have plenty of room," he told them. "Why not come and stay a week with us?" He hugged them both. Reverend King became their teacher, mentor, and dear friend. The StorySingers took his advice, added his style of audience involvement to their presentations, and became a hit wherever they performed.

AND AWAY WE GO

The shrill ringing clashed with the humming, machine-gun-like stuttering of the sewing machine. Verna hurried to answer the phone. She'd been sewing since early morning, and the sound startled her. Norman was at an appointment with an event organizer for a funny-sounding festival, "Harvey Field Corn Roast and Fly-In," where they were scheduled to appear.

"Hello?...Why, Reverend Furman. How nice of you to call...What?...The annual picnic?...Yes, the last Sunday of next month...featured entertainment?" Verna's face glowed as if suddenly framed in a sunbeam's spotlight. Her eyes flashed with glee, lit from within by excitement's spark. "Why, yes, of course... Yes...We'd be delighted to perform." She smiled. "A love offering?...Sure...Of course...Yes, a love offering would be...well...just lovely. Thank you. Good bye." She cradled the receiver and stood in the kitchen next to the phone for a moment. *Wow! Performing at The Way's annual picnic!...featured entertainment we'll be, he said...featured entertainers at one of the biggest events in one of the biggest churches in Seattle!...oh, thank You, God!...oh, my bread!* She checked the bread dough and realized it would be ready for the oven in a half hour. Such amazing news she would have to tell Norman when he returned.

Back at the sewing machine, she started its needle's *tat-tat-tat-tatting* again and carefully stitched white lace on a new patchwork skirt pieced together from teal satin and black velvet. She smiled and hummed the song she'd written for Norman. *...Come on let's fly this universe...for together we are...our wings!*

Initially, people at the picnic assumed the show was only for children, but adults drifted near, equally spellbound as the ancient phrase "Once Upon a Time" worked its magic on them, too. The homey fireplace, flanked by two maple and tapestry rockers, created a welcoming space that beckoned everyone. People sat on blankets, beach towels, or just on the lush green grass. Some unfolded webbed lawn chairs, stretched out their legs, and settled comfortably. Norman and Verna's ability to project their voices to reach even the furthest edge of the audience, the charming puppets, and Michelle's music transported the listeners into enchantment. Wonderland indeed.

As they were "breaking the set" after the show, a man wearing a black beret approached. "Hi, there. My name is Roderick Reardon." He grinned and stuck out his hand. Norman took it, and they shook. "So, you two are the, uh, The

StorySingers, is that right?" Norman and Verna nodded, smiled, and kept folding and packing. "I book talent for the Seattle Center. You know the center stage in the center stage area?" Norman stopped packing. He smiled and said, "Yes. I do know it. How can we help you, sir?" Roderick was fascinated by the muppet-style puppets Verna was carefully storing in the puppet case. As the latches closed, he tore his gaze away and returned his attention to Norman.

"I would like to book your show. As you may know, The Seattle Center produces an annual Children's Festival, and I think you'd fit in very well." Norman's smile widened. "Well, thank you, sir. Please follow me to our van. I'd be glad to show you our portfolio and discuss possibilities." He glanced over his shoulder. "You okay here for a minute, Verna?" She nodded in return, curious about what the stranger wanted, and grateful they had a photographic compilation of their personal entertainment product. Their dear friend, Clarice, besides their wedding shots, had provided promotional photographs of them to flesh out their StorySingers' portfolio. Clarice was a solid foundation of their launching pad when they began their adventure. She remained a close friend for the rest of her life.

Later at home over grilled cheese sandwiches and pickles they discussed the picnic. Norman smiled at his wife. "Wasn't this an unexpected blessing? I had no idea what a 'Love Offering' entailed. Apparently, everybody there contributed. I do believe we made the van payment today. In just one show!"

"Tell me about the man in the black beret. What was all that about?" Verna sipped her tea and glanced at Norman.

"Well, Roderick Reardon is the talent booking agent for The Seattle Center's Center Stage venue. And, my love, that means we are going to be performing at the Seattle Center for this year's Children's Festival! This is what I have hoped for."

Verna took a bite and chewed thoughtfully. She reached for a pickle slice and said, "Which show?"

Norman patted her hand. "We're going to design it, and you, my lovely, are going to learn some more stories." He rose and opened his briefcase and handed her a sheaf of typewritten pages.

Her eyes widened. "This is quite a show. Looks like a lot to learn." Doubtfully, she laid the outline down and took a bite of pickle, forgetting she held a sandwich half in the other hand. "Is there any music in it?" She was wondering about learning new songs.

Norman took her hand and looked lovingly across the table at her. "Not yet," he smiled. "But I think there will be. We'll set up, start rehearsing, see what new ideas may come, and who knows? Maybe you'll write a new song just for that show. And we may think of a completely different theme and stories. After all, it's ours to create. And I love creating with you!" He leaned across the table and kissed her soundly on the mouth. "Oooh...a pickle-flavored kiss. My favorite!" He winked and went back to his own sandwich.

The Seattle Center's Children's Festival was the first of numerous performances in which The StorySingers appeared upon The Center's center stage. Norman and Verna became "regulars" in Roderick Reardon's stable of entertainers. Their initial presentation was designed around animal songs and stories kids loved and adults fondly remembered from childhood. A sing-a-long with "Old McDonald Had A Farm" began the show, then moved into their adaptation of "Chicken Little." Verna operated the chicken puppet while Norman, the "panicky farmer" in front of the fireplace screen, interacted with other puppets, including a frog unconcerned if the sky *did* fall since he was quite safe under his lily pad, thank you, and did the farmer want to join him there? They then involved the audience in lively singing of "Froggy Went A-Courtin'" and segued into "The Frog Prince." Verna, the "beautiful princess," kissed Norman's frog puppet who, lo and behold!, emerged in the person of Norman from behind the fireplace as *The Handsome Prince!* Next was a sing-a-long of "The Teddy Bears Picnic," followed by the story of "Goldilocks and the Three Bears." Verna, of course, was Goldilocks while Norman worked the bear puppets from behind the fireplace. They ended the show with Verna leading "This Old Man (Knick-Knack-Paddy-Whack-Give-A-Dog-A-Bone!)" while Norman's dog puppet popped up behind the fireplace every time the audience "gave-a-dog-a-bone" in the song. The show was a template of the style in which they interacted with each other as performers and puppeteers. It was a smashing success!

"Harvey Field Corn Roast and Fly-in, huh? What is that over there where those planes are lined up?" asked Verna from the passenger seat. She had had her fill of driving, and happily gave Norman the keys whenever they were going to an engagement.

"Wellll...near as I can tell, it seems to be a grass landing strip next to the cornfield. Once a year, they hold a sort of festival, with an entertainment stage, and people fly in for it. Or, maybe people fly in just to show off their personal airplanes. At any rate, they have an entertainment stage, and 'The StorySingers' are featured on it." He grinned. "That's us!"

Harvey Field consisted of a low, one-story, freshly-beige-painted, three-room *(a "waiting room" with one long folding table, several folding metal chairs and a couple of webbed lawn ones, a water fountain, a wall clock, and a vending machine – an "office" with its own wall clock, a desk and its accoutrements, plus a couch – and a bathroom)* concrete block terminal with two large horn loudspeakers mounted on its roof. There were a couple of blue-covered, open-sided, carport-type hangers beside the terminal with a small orange airplane under one and a nondescript gray pickup belonging to the terminal manager under the other. The grass landing strip was in front of the terminal, and a flat grassy area served as the taxiing zone for airplanes taking off and landing. About an acre of cleared space was reserved for the entertainment stage *(an old, rusted flatbed truck)* and for folks who had come out to enjoy the festivities.

All of this was surrounded by a huge cornfield whose stalks were laden with green-enclosed ears ripe for picking. It was a gently-warm-but-not-too-hot sunny day, blue sky, a few white, puffy clouds floating by, gentle breeze – a perfect late-summer day for a fly-in festival in a cornfield; a unique festival, to be sure. To the organizers' knowledge, this was the only cornfield in the nation with an airport in the middle of it where airplane aficionados wearing "Corn Roast" tee shirts gathered once a year to pick corn as they gnawed roasted corn cobs between puffs of smoking corn cob pipes while craning their necks and straining their ears to see and hear entertainers on an antique flatbed truck bed while single-engine piper cubs buzzed low over their heads and vintage biplanes looped figure eights in the sky as the terminal's two roof loudspeakers shrieked "He made it!" when Harvey Field's mascot dressed as the imaginary rabbit of the Pulitzer prize-winning play landed his pink ultralight in front of the terminal.

Besides the two large horn loudspeakers on the terminal's roof, there was a sound system for entertainers. It consisted of an ancient box amp and one stand microphone set up on the bed of the flatbed truck; several plugged-together extension cords snaked their way from the amp down from the truck bed to an outlet inside the terminal, the cord line covered with various towels and throw rugs with notes of "Watch Your Step!" taped to them.

The flatbed's stage featured some wobbly, cracked, broken boards from which a few nails had worked their way loose. To get up on it, a five rung metal ladder was attached to the truck's side. Norman ascended first; Verna passed him Michelle and her guitar stand. For herself, it was clumsy going with her long skirt, but she finally managed. From the elevation of the flatbed, the view was amazing.

Beside and behind the terminal, small colorful airplanes were parked wing-to-wing, shining in the summer sun, waiting to take their places in the taxiing area. Next to the stage were several cooking stations where huge vats of cooking corn gave off a rather sweet aroma mixed with the fragrant smell of corn cob pipe tobacco smoke. A few vendor tents lined the perimeter of the cleared area. People moved like so many ants in the corn rows as they picked corn to take home, and every cooking station had a line of people waiting to buy the huge ears of bright yellow corn to eat while watching the airplanes and the entertainment. There was quite a crowd, consisting mostly of families. The air was filled with sounds of whizzing and roaring airplanes. To Verna it felt odd preparing to sing to a crowd of people gnawing on corn while planes buzzed overhead as the shrill sound system from the terminal's roof horns intermittently announced things like "May we draw your attention to the 1975 red-and-white Cessna 172 now taking off to circle the field" as a Cessna 182 Skylane bellowed in beside it for a landing, and vendors shouted "Hey, Fly-in tee shirts! Getcher Fly-In tee shirt!," "Corncob pipes! Here ya go, corncob pipes!," and "Hot corn! Hot corn! Getcher hot corn right cheer!" Actually, it not only *felt* odd to Verna…it *was* odd! Still, it was a paid performance. They did not set up the puppet screen for this appearance, as that would have been an exercise in the utmost of futilities! They planned to present sing-along songs and puppet-less stories similar to "The Tailor."

As that red-and-white Cessna 172 buzzed the flatbed, Verna plugged her sound block into the guitar and the cord's end into the amplifier provided. Since there was but one microphone, she and Norman stood close in order to be heard and launched into their introduction. At the sound of the theme song, heads turned in their direction, and the crowd began to ooze like a giant amoeba toward them. Verna felt hysterical giggles starting to rise at the sight of all those open mouths chomping corn. She managed to quash her hysteria, barely, and commenced the first story. Another airplane droned over the crowd, the noise blotting out what they were saying. Shouts of "We can't hear you!" floated up to the stage. Verna looked at Norman with eyebrows raised in a silent question *what can we do here?*

"Thanks, everyone," he said. "We're going to change the situation here a little bit. We're going to come down there where you are. Bear with us a minute." Norman smiled at the crowd, gestured toward the air and the planes flying close by, and shrugged. Verna had already unplugged the amp cord, picked up the guitar stand, slid Michelle around to her back, and climbed down the metal ladder. The crowd, agape at the change, stopped chewing their corn. Standing on the grass in front of the audience, the two colorfully-dressed StorySingers once again began their show, this time without amplification. It became an intimate presentation as the crowd gathered close around them, and they interspersed sing-along songs "a la maniere de Charles King," their dear friend and mentor. Charles taught them to adjust to circumstances, to adapt to an audience, to "go with the flow," as it were. These were certainly peculiar conditions in which to perform – planes taking off and landing close by, terminal roof horns blaring, vendors hawking – yet The StorySingers delivered a very successful performance. The crowd, between bites of corn and puffs of pipes, sang along with the songs, enjoyed the stories, and applauded at the finish. In addition to their performance check, the organizer offered them a bushel of corn to take home. They ate corn-on-the-cob for a month!

Back in the van, they looked at each other and at last the hysterical giggles were let loose. "Did you ever see such a thing?" gasped Verna. "It was like trying to sing to a bunch of hogs chomping on their corn!" She giggled louder. Norman laughed, too. "Well, we certainly couldn't compete with the noise of the airplanes with the small sound system they provided, so I just thought it would be better to go ahead like we did at the church picnic." Verna wiped laughter tears and smiled at her husband. "You were right. Now, everyone in that crowd is going to think of The StorySingers every time they eat corn! And I will think of *this* every time I do!"

Besides flatbed truck beds, Verna and Norman would perform on sites of flat, bare ground, church daises, community event tent platforms, school stages, within living rooms, luxurious state-of-the-art performing art centers, conference halls, and television and radio studios. They would travel the United States from coast to coast and border to border as they presented their special brand of entertainment – original stories and songs, adaptations of classic tales, specialized shows for holidays, and custom-created shows upon request. They would forget some of the venues in which they appeared. But the "Harvey Field Corn Roast and Fly In" remained an oddly fond memory for them both.

STORYSONGS AND MIRACLES

Hallmarks of The StorySingers were their original StorySongs, powerful pieces wherever they were performed. A storysong began as a story told – with Verna's underlying guitar accompaniment – and smoothly transitioned into a story sung. Storysongs utlized minimal personal props and no puppetry. Inspiration for them came from many sources – dreams, random flashes of Creativity's Muse, or thoughtful searching for a stiumlating spark. Reverend Furman of The Way preached a sermon on butterflies which sparked the storysong of "The Little Wooly Bug." His talk, entitled "A New Creation," was based upon 2 Corinthians 5:17 – "...old things are passed away; behold, all things are become new."

"We can learn much from a little wooly bug's transition into a beautiful butterfly," he said. "Caterpillars can only crawl upon the ground; their vision downward, not toward the sky. They really think only of themselves as they busily gorge on leaves, many times destroying plants upon which they feed. They take and do not give. But then they form themselves into a chrysalis, a cocoon. It is there, within, they are transformed into a beautiful creature of the air, no longer crawling upon the ground but flying free, eyes skyward, pollinating plants upon which they once fed, spreading new life, giving instead of taking. Their old are passed away, and, behold, all has become new. So it is when we stop gorging on outward earthly distractions, wrap ourselves within God's Cocoon, live in Christ and Christ in us, and allow God to work His Wonders within our beings. We emerge as a new spirit, eyes upon heaven, spreading His Love, His Life, flying free as the beautiful creation He means us to be. Our Father sees us as a butterfly, not as a little wooly bug."

"Hmmm...little wooly bug to a cocoon and then a butterfly...certainly an evolution in one lifetime," said Norman as he and Verna returned home after church. "Did you play with caterpillars when you were little?"

"Yes, I suppose so. But I called them little wooly bugs like Reverend Furman did in his sermon." Verna retrieved the jar of sun tea from the porch as they went inside the manufactured home, poured it into a pitcher, and placed it in the refrigerator to chill. "I wonder if they dream while inside their cocoons...do they know they'll wake up with wings one day?" She put a pan on the stove with sugar and water to prepare simple syrup to sweeten the tea.

Norman reached for her and drew her to him. "We should write something about what little wooly bugs dream about."

"Or maybe a song about a little wooly bug who wakes up amazed to find himself changed into a creature with beautiful wings." Thoughtfully, she stirred the syrup, added it to the pitcher, replaced the pitcher in the fridge, and reached for Michelle. She and Norman began their process of "Once upon a time there was a little wooly bug"…and the storysong of a little caterpillar who found wings he never knew he had began to emerge.

"Hmmm…it needs special costuming…a cocoon…and wings…how in the world are we ever going to make wings? I do have some fabric, but none of it can be wings. And what about the cocoon? How would we make that?" The phone rang.

"Hi, Clarice." Norman paused and listened. "Tonight? Well, sure we can. Love your stir-fries. Thanks. See you at seven."

Delicious aromas whiffed through Clarice's house. Confetti rice was in the cooker, and Verna smelled sweet peppers. In the kitchen Shanti diced carrots on a counter, and Clarice placed Verna in front of a mound of sweet onions to dice. As vegetables were added to a wok, Norman told Clarice about their new piece, "The Little Wooly Bug."

"Y'know," Clarice considered, "I think I may have something you could use for your wings. I'll be right back. Here, Norman, you stir." She handed him chopsticks to stir the wok and disappeared behind the basement door.

When she returned, Shanti and Verna were dishing up dinner. Clarice carried a partial bolt of blue chiffon, one of yellow chiffon, and a folded bundle of black broadcloth. She sketched her idea for the wings and cocoon. "I'd sew it, but I don't have my machine anymore," she said as she slid the sketched design across the table to Verna.

The four friends smiled at one another. "You guys are fun!" exclaimed Shanti. She waved her chopsticks at the sketch. "I can see Norman wearing this get up, and he'd be a perfect little wooly bug. Probably a bit grumpy, though, at having to crawl on the ground," she giggled. "But, oh, when he drops that black cocoon and spreads out his new wings!"

Huh!…a <u>grumpy</u> little wooly bug…yeah!

"Once upon a time there was a fuzzy little caterpillar who was so covered with fuzz that he looked just like a little wooly bug," Verna, alone on stage, commenced the story as Michelle softly accompanied her. "Now this little caterpillar took being a bug very seriously."

"Yeah! It ain't easy bein' a bug, especially a little wooly one!" a black-cloak-wrapped Norman grumpily grumped as he entered the stage.

"Sometimes rainbow-colored butterflies would dip and swoop and swirl around the little caterpillar," Verna continued. "They called to him to come up and fly with them. It's great fun!"

"No, sir! Not me! I'm stayin' right here on the ground! You ain't getting' me up in one of them things! Hunh-uh!"

"You'll see, the butterflies laughed," said Verna. "You will change someday because you, too, have wings inside."

"Bah! Nothin' inside me except leaves and grass! Few twigs for roughage, maybe. My life will never change!"

Thus the told story began. It changed into a song as Norman, bent over in his black cocoon, groused around the stage, and Verna began singing, "I never sang much about little wooly bugs, never gave 'em too much thought. When I thought about 'em much, I just said 'Ugh!' Didn't think about the lessons they taught."

As the storysong progressed, Norman, completely shocked at his "evolving transition," twirled around and around in his cocoon cape until he dropped it and unfolded enormous blue and yellow wings on wire frames. Then Norman sang, "Once was I a little wooly bug, didn't know that I had wings. When told I could fly I just said 'unh-uh' and stayed with familiar things…I dared to look deep inside me. There was a pair of beautiful wings…So claim your wings! They're already yours for the taking!"

Together Norman and Verna finished singing in harmony," "Cause you can fly on your very own wings!"

It was a *Big Piece!*...a hugely triumphant piece...one that ended on a gloriously victorious note! It was a piece that vividly expressed Verna's surmounting the drudges of Welfare, miseries of an inexplicable, high-risk pregnancy, toils of nursing school, heartbreaks of losing children, dregs of catatonia, distresses of failed marriages, and all obstacles overcome on her journey of becoming the strong, vibrant, talented StorySinger whose "season had arrived in its time," unfolding her own wings to fly to heights of which she had never dreamed.

It was also a miraculous piece, one that saved a life.

"The Little Wooly Bug" was a "finishing piece," one that Verna and Norman used for ending presentations on a jubilant note. It was extremely well received wherever performed. As professional entertainers, they toured somewhat circuitously, returning to a venue periodically. Once they appeared in a fairly small Oregon church, A 30ish-looking woman and a teeanaged girl entered after the concert started and sat at the very back. The teenager, obviously unhappy, sat with her arms crossed throughout the presentation, looking about as grumpy as the fuzzy caterpillar in the storysong. That particular concert finished with "The Little Wooly Bug." As audience members gathered around Verna and Norman at their product table, the woman bought a cassette tape featuring "The Little Wooly Bug," and she and the teenager quickly left.

Two years later The StorySingers returned to that same church. The woman and teenager were there again; this time the young girl looked happy and participated in the concert's sing-a-longs. After the presentation, the woman and girl approached Norman and Verna.

"We were here last time," the woman said. "I'm Roberta. This is my daughter, Carrie. She didn't want to come then, but I forced her to. After the concert when we got home, she told me she had planned to commit suicide that day and showed me the bottle of pills she was going to take. Your story about the little wooly bug changed her mind."

"Yes," Carrie replied."You made me realize I had wings inside me, too. I could be happy. I didn't have to die. Just like the caterpillar, I could change. My mom bought one of your tapes, the one with 'The Little Wooly Bug' on it. I got a blank tape and recorded that over and over on it. And I listened to that tape until it was worn out. That's what changed my mind. That's why I'm still alive."

Oh, my! thought Verna. *Paul wrote something about great are the mysteries of God. He does work in mysterious ways His wonders to perform! We have been involved in a miracle, and we didn't even know it until now!*

Richard Brothers, associate minister and youth pastor of The Way, was quite popular with the congregation, and the spacious sanctuary was usually packed for his twice-monthly sermons. But Richard was moving on as he had accepted a call to be senior minister of a congregation in Huntington Beach, California. That was fine with Richard, as he was a surfer dude, a quintessential blonde, blue-eyed, deeply tanned, solid, washboard-abbed surfboarder who just happened to be a minister in one of Seattle's largest churches. Now he wouldn't have to drive as far to find nice, A-framed waves on whose lips he could "get some serious air on his long, big board" before slapping back down on the wave's face to ride it to its beach break. Puget Sound and the Strait of Juan de Fuca didn't lend themselves very well to surfing. So Richard was happy, estatic even, to move on to greener pastures – and bigger waves.

Yet he understood his departure would be deeply distressing, perhaps traumatizing, to The Way's congregation. Many of them looked to him – depended upon him – as their spiritual leader, their religious rock. He correctly surmised his leaving would rip a hole in some psyches. What to do? How could he make his parting as painless as possible and also remind them of their own inner strengths, their innate resources? He decided to break the news a month in advance so people could have some time to adjust as well as counsel with him. He would preach a sermon about him moving on while encouraging congregants to be strong in themselves. He chose 2 Timothy 1:7 as his text. "For God hath not given us the spirit of fear; but of power, and of love, and of a sound mind." *Yes! There is no need to fear my departure. You are always immersed in God's Power, His Love, and His Strength. I only remind you of Christ within you through whom you can be strong, through whom you can do all things, through whom you can release me without fear.*

But Richard needed a "set-up," an entre into his sermon, something to open hearts to be receptive to his message. By this time in their career, Verna and Norman were well known in the region, especially in The Way as they had presented special music for Sunday services, meditations for Vespers, and several full StorySinger presentatons for church events. Richard made an appointment with them in his office and explained his thoughts.

Bartholomew Bigglesworth, the small boy who lived in The Enchanted Village where sometimes Magical People come along to play with him, introduced himself to Verna in a dream. She introduced him to Norman who said, "Ah! Yes, Bartholomew! I believe he wears speckled shoes sometimes." So was the storysong, "Speckled Shoes," born. It was the perfect lead-in to Richards's departing sermon.

"Bartholomew was a 'boy's boy,' full of wonder and light-hearted liveliness," so Verna began telling the story and plinking cheerful notes from Michelle. "He loved to be with magical people who helped him feel magical himself. But sometimes there just wasn't anyone around, and he got bored and, at times, even fearful."

As little Bartholomew, Norman continued. "It sure is fun when magical people come along. They make me feel really good when they're around. But when they go away, I'm here all by myself with nothing to do. I get lonesome. Sometimes I get scared. I wish I was a magical person and could go magical places and do magical things."

The Blue Fairy –a flitty-flighty-figedity-twitchedy persona of Verna's – appeared as Verna donned a blue, star-spangled, rigid-cone-shaped hat and picked up a large, blue, sequin-studded, soft-fabric purse. As Norman introduced the Blue Fairy, he explained "People were never quite certain exactly where the Blue Fairy was because she was able to become invisible and visible at will. Many times this condition caused the Blue Fairy herself not to be quite certain of exactly where she was. However, on this day, she just happened to be running up a sunbeam near Bartholomew and overheard his wish. She popped into visibility right in front of him."

"My goodness! Hello, Bartholomew!"

"Oh! Blue Fairy! You surprised me!"

"Well, I surprise myself sometimes when I discover where I am. Did I just hear you make a wish?"

"Yeah, Blue Fairy. Sometimes magical people come along, and they make me feel real good inside while they're here. But then they go away again, and I feel all sad and empty inside. I wish I was a magical person and could go magical places and do magical things."

"Why, Bartholomew, I have my Blue Fairy Magic Bag, and there's always something magical for little boys who need some. Goodness me, let's see what's in here."

The Blue Fairy rummaged in her bag and pulled out a pair of white shoes dotted with multi-colored sequins.

"Oh, Blue Fairy. Those are just shoes!"

"Yes, but they're not just ordinary shoes, Bartholomew. These are speckled shoes! See how they shine and sparkle! Put them on."

"Yeah! I'll just take off my other shoes and put these on. Oh, they feel really good, Blue Fairy! Oh, I can wiggle my toes!"

"Bartholomew, in those shoes you can run up a sunbeam, skate down a rainbow, skip 'round the sun, leapfrog the moon, dance on a cloud, hop from star to star, walk on the wind, and travel where you choose in your flashing, dashing, stupendously smashing, sparkling speckled shoes."

So the story told became a story sung as Bartholomew and the Blue Fairy sang of speckled shoes that reminds us all of our own inner strengths that need no others to vindicate us, our magic within that allows us to overcome fears and doubts that sometimes sneak in to steal away our peace, happiness, and inner self-esteem – speckled shoes that, when we put them on, let us travel where we choose, be who we are meant to be, and remind us of our Christ-strength within.

"Speckled Shoes," a lively, bouncy storysong, was exactly the vehicle Richard needed to set up his leave-taking sermon. It became a staple in The StorySingers' repertoire, presented in numerous venues.

One of those venues was a weekend motivational retreat in the Midwest. Verna and Norman were booked to facilitate a storytelling workshop followed with a presentation by workshop participants. The workshop included participants creating their own speckled shoes by gluing sequins on donated hospital operating room disposable paper shoe covers, the kind worn by OR personnel. Workshop participants would be a back-up chorus for Verna and Norman as they all sang the storysong's chorus, "I can skate down a rainbow, dance on a cloud, or hop from star to star. I can walk on the wind, run up a sunbeam, or tiptoe near and far. I can skip 'round the sun, leapfrog the moon, or travel where I choose in my flashing, dashing, stupendously smashing, sparkling speckled shoes." The presentation was fantastic! Another successful booking!

After the retreat, The StorySingers were engaged to present a mid-week evening concert in a Chicago church. It was an intimate venue, the church's social hall, and the audience's front row was relatively close to the low platform on which Verna and Norman performed. There were three women sitting together in the front row directly in front of the platform.

Unbeknownst to either Verna or Norman, a pair of sequined shoe covers from the workshop had somehow been placed in the Blue Fairy's Magic Bag along with the prop speckled shoes she pulled out to give to Norman's Bartholomew character. The StorySingers began "Speckled Shoes," the final piece of the evening's presentation, and when Verna removed the prop shoes, the shoe covers flew out of the bag like glittering confetti pieces and twinkled slowly down to the feet of the woman sitting between the other two.

As soon as the show ended, Verna and Norman stepped down to the woman before she could arise, apologized for their "prop malfunction," and Norman presented her with the two speckled shoe covers saying, "These must be yours! We didn't know they were in the bag, but they must have been waiting for you!"

It turned out the woman's daughter had been murdered a year ago on this very date. The woman had not ventured outside of her house at all for the past year. On this night her two friends had convinced her to attend The StorySingers' concert. The "Speckled Shoes" storysong, plus the flying, floating shoe covers, brought soothing closure to her hurting heart. "Your song spoke to me. Showed me I'm really strong inside. And these covers, *my* speckled shoes, must be a message from my daughter's spirit to tell me I'll never be alone. She's got me covered. God's got me covered! Thank you so much!"

A message from a murdered daughter's spirit? Or a miracle, another great mystery of God? Whatever it was, it was a most memorable event!

Upon completion of their song, "The Christmas Star," and after savoring those silent seconds of enchantment following it, Verna and Norman continued their show on the Seattle Center's Center Stage as they helped launch the Seattle Center's 1990 "Celebrating Christmas" season-long event.

The show ended with Verna as Mrs. Santa reading "The Night Before Christmas" as she sat in her rocker next to a small, decorated, multi-colored-light-lit Christmas tree standing on a small table by the soft-sculptured fireplace. When Santa "comes down the chimney with a bound," Norman in full Santa Claus regalia entered from behind the fireplace screen where he donned his costume. A transitional piece between the ending of "The Christmas Star" and Santa's appearance allowed him time to change. It was their storysong of "The Smallest Polar Bear" which featured their song "It's A Rainbow Christmas."

The story told began as Norman explained that the very first Christmas tree was decorated by Mrs. Santa as Verna's Mrs Santa wrapped a prop plastic popcorn string around the unlit tree.

Mrs. Santa: "Oh, and I'll just catch some snowflakes and put them on the tree. And some icicles from the eaves of Santa's workshop. Oh, my, they look so pretty.."

Norman: "And a star from the sky, the Christmas Star, came down to sit on the very top of the tree. But something was missing. It lacked color. And so the smallest polar bear ran up to Mrs. Santa, and he said...*(as smallest polar bear)* Oh, Mrs. Santa, Mrs. Santa. Can I go to the rainbow patch and pull down a rainbow and wrap it around the tree? Can I, huh? Please?"

Mrs. Santa: "Why, of course, you can, smallest polar bear. That would be so lovely. Be careful now. Don't slip on the ice and fall. You'll break the rainbow if you do."

Norman: "And so the smallest polar bear ran to the rainbow patch and pulled down the brightest rainbow he could find. He folded it in his arms and ran back to Mrs. Santa. But he did slip on the ice and fall and broke the rainbow into hundreds of pieces….*(as smallest polar bear)* Oh, Mrs. Santa, look. Oh, I broke the rainbow into hundreds of pieces. Oh, Mrs. Santa…*(crying)*

Mrs. Santa: "Oh, don't cry, smallest polar bear. It's all right. It's ok. Look. Let's gather up the pieces and put them on the tree. Look. There's a blue one, and there's a red one, and over there's a green one. Gather them all, and we'll put them on the tree like this."

Norman and Verna "gathered up the pieces of the broken rainbow" and placed them on the tree. "Look, smallest polar bear!" Verna surreptitiously plugged in a concealed string of multi-colored lights in the tree to a hidden extension cord attached to the table. The plastic popcorned, icicled, star-topped tree burst forth into a kaleidoscope of brilliant rainbow color! *(Audiences invariably "oohed" at this bit of stage magic!)* "See, smallest polar bear. It's a rainbow Christmas tree!" "Oh, wow, Mrs. Santa! It's a rainbow Christmas!"

Norman: "And that is how rainbow Christmas tree lights came to be on Christmas trees."

While Norman slipped behind the puppet screen, Verna began the story sung as she positioned Michelle over her shoulder, softly began playing, and serenely sang, "It's a rainbow Christmas, a rainbow Christmas world. It's a rainbow Christmas, a rainbow Christmas world…One Christmas time there stood a tree in dark and cold of winter night; it symbolized for all to see the baby's birth who brought us light…Then the smallest polar bear saw a rainbow in the sky and pulled it down from way up there to shine as night was passing by…It's a rainbow Christmas, a rainbow Christmas world…" The gentle song mesmerized audiences, enraptured them in its charm, enthralled them as they swayed to its soothing rhythm and quietly sang along. It was a wonderful piece to segue into Mrs. Santa's calm reading of "The Night Before Christmas" and a masterful balance to Santa's explosive appearance at the show's upbeat ending.

After the standing ovation and accolades died away and the audience melted into the mumbling mix of shoppers seeping in and out of shops, an elderly, white-haired man stood alone among the empty chairs. He stepped up to the platform stage. Tears tracked the furrows in his face, overflowing from his brimming eyes. Norman and Verna stood at the platform's edge to greet him. He reached up, took a hand of theirs in one of his, and said, "Thank you so much. You have healed Christmas for me. When I was a child, you see, my parents expected me to fetch the box of Christmas tree lights from the attic every year. Decorating the tree was supposed to be a fun family thing, and my mission, my *job*, was to bring down the box of lights from the attic from the time I was old enough to do it. I was supposed to enjoy it. My daddy always sternly warned me to be careful, to not fall and break the lights. Well, one Christmas I tripped on the last stair step, fell, dropped the box, and landed on top of it. That broke the lights. And instead of being worried about how I was, both my daddy and mom got really mad at me, screamed at me, told me how stupid and clumsy I was, and sent me to my room. I decided then I'd never decorate another Christmas tree if I could help it, and

Christmas has always been a sad time for me until right now. Your sweet story and song about the little bear breaking the rainbow like I once broke the lights has healed my heart. I never thought it could be. You have given me a miracle. Thank you so much."

What began as a filler piece to cover Norman getting into his Santa costume became a magical, cherished part of The StorySingers' Christmas Show. Almost every time "The Smallest Polar Bear" was told and "A Rainbow Christmas" was sung, audience members would report some type of "Christmas healing" for themselves. The storysong touched a yearning for the sweetness, the kindness, the compassion of Christmas as it was meant to be. It was a miracle of inspiration, another mysterious way in which God performed one of His Wonders.

EXPECT A MIRACLE

EXPECT A MIRACLE bumper stickers began appearing on vehicles in 1990. Verna and Norman placed one on both the front and rear bumpers of their black van. "You are a miracle to me, Verna," Norman said as they kneeled and stuck one on the front bumper.

"Oh, you are one of the greatest miracles I've ever received, Sweetheart," Verna replied with a smile. Her eyes moistened with tears. "I've told you before about being in Mesquite Valley as a catatonic patient. Well, to have been locked inside myself in that silence for so long was nightmarish." She sniffled a little and straightened up. Norman stood up next to her and laid a hand on her arm. "I came out of that silence because of a music therapist, Tom Nation. He played 'Amazing Grace' on his guitar, and my heart heard it. I followed it out of the silence and, well, got myself back." Norman put his arms around her and hugged her. "Then I got a guitar of my own, and, much to my amazement, I started writing songs."

Verna looked deep into his eyes.

"I didn't know why I started writing them. Or how they came. But that instant I sat down next to you in church, I think I understood what God was doing. All of a sudden it was like...*boom!*...there you were. And here we are, our miracles to each other." As they knelt down to affix the sticker to the rear bumper, she continued. "And now, going to Susanna's wedding is just as big of a miracle! And you've booked us into performances all along the way. You've made it so that we can go. Oh, I do love you so."

Norman smiled and rose as he helped Verna stand. "I love you, too! And we begin our tour to Tucson tomorrow! Presenting our Christmas Show to kick off the Seattle Center's 1990 'Celebrating Christmas' was a great way to start the tour, don't you think? I mean, we go down through Oregon, California, Phoenix, the wedding in Tucson, and then on to Florida and up the east coast and back to Seattle through the northern states. Wow!" Norman's face was ablaze with joy. And possibilities.

"Yes! I can't wait to see Susanna again! My little girl all grown up. A bride! And you made it happen, Norman! Just like our very first engagement when you opened the yellow pages to day care centers and started calling each one until you got a yes."

"Yeah! Fifty dollars per show we charged then, thanks to your prophetic dream." Norman grinned. "Now look at us! Three hundred and seventy five dollars per show, and the calls keep coming in!"

They hugged each other and went inside their peaceful home.

Anne Marie and Patrick Williams &
Francene and Chastain R. Boone II
request the honor of your presence
at the marriage of their children
Susanna Marie Williams
and
Chastain "Chase" R. Boone III
Sunday, the first of January
nineteen ninety one
at five o'clock in the afternoon
The Chapel at Old Tucson
Tucson, Arizona

In March, nine months ago, Verna received a most welcome surprise – an invitation to Susanna's wedding in Tucson. It was in 1975, 15 years past, when Verna last saw her two daughters, Veronica, now 26, and Susanna, now 22. Fifteen years ago their stepmother, now legally their adoptive mother, Anne Marie, ordered Verna out of their lives forever. Verna had not seen them since that day when she, with the best of intentions, picked up Veronica and Susanna after school and drove them home. She wanted to talk with Veronica about a dream in which Verna's dreamself saw her daughter pour some vodka into her school thermos. Anne Marie had exploded in fury at Verna's unannounced, unexpected, and what she considered to be an irresponsible pickup of the girls. "They are *my* daughters now, do you hear me, Verna?" her face gone dark red, her shoulders quivering with rage. "You are *not* to see them! *Not ever!*"

Since that time Verna remained in limited contact with Susanna while she was still in school via clandestine communication with letters exchanged through her old friend Janice Sawtelle. After graduation, there had been very few letters, and an occasional card. At Susanna's request, it was Janice who conveyed Susanna's wedding invitation to Verna.

Veronica, who ran away from her Tucson home when she was but thirteen years old, appeared in what Verna referred to as her "Dream Travels." Thanks to those nocturnal occurences. She felt her daughter was all right.

"He's a person, damn you! Don'tchu get it? A person! Ya don't just…just… scoop 'im up like garbage in the street!" Veronica, in jeans and denim jacket, holding the straps of her denim backpack in one hand and leashes to two dogs in the other, strode back and forth in front of a small yellow nylon tent pitched in what appeared to be a city park. "He died, okay? He's dead. I woke up next to 'im and he was…was..all..cold like." She sniffled and wiped her nose with her jacket sleeve. "He was my friend! He had a name! His name is Walt,,,never Walter…just…Walt."

Verna's dreamself watched anxiously as Veronica appeared to stop and stand guard in front of the little tent.. Red and blue lights from police cruisers flickered disco-like over the scene. Verna saw a uniformed police woman advancing cautiously toward her daughter. Veronica, apparently exhausted, sank down slowly onto the cold cement sidewalk. She sobbed aloud, her face red and tear-streaked. Her blue bandanna clung crookedly to her head, light brown hair, matted and greasy, hanging down her back. The female officer spoke gently, reassurance in her voice.

"Just let us get to him, okay?" Her expression was concerned. "The coroner has been called. Let us help you." She advanced a slow step, and the big red-and-white dog barked thunderously and lunged at her, to protect Veronica. Small yips and barks emanated from the tent's interior. Veronica looked up.

"That will be Baxter. The small terrier I saw inside Walt's jacket," thought Verna's dreamself.

The officer spoke softly. "Please, Miss. Just step aside and let us help. We only want to help." Her voice was calm and gentle. Veronica remained seated, but slowly nodded her head. "Kitty, sit! Lady, down!" The two dogs obediently followed her commands. She called toward the tent, "Baxter! It's okay. This lady is gonna help Wa…Wal…Walt." She choked on the name.

The female officer knelt and laid a hand on Veronica's shoulder. "You're exhausted. Let's get you a meal and bed for the night, okay?" Veronica clutched the leashes harder, her knuckles whitened under the grime. She nodded. A male officer exited the tent, carefully carrying a small bundle of fury. The little black-and-white dog, held at arm's length, was snarling and snapping,"Baxter, is it?" he asked. Veronica nodded. "Yes. Put him in Walt's backpack, and I'll take 'im with me. He's okay. Just little..and..and…kinda nervous. Y'know? Walt carried him all the time in his jacket to help keep his chest warm." The female officer rose and reached for the small dog. Another officer entered the tent and emerged with a black backpack, unzipping it as he walked.

Verna's dreamself watched her daughter's tear-streaked face turn away as two men in black jumpsuits emerged from a black van. The coroners. Veronica yelled at them. "You be careful with 'im, y'hear? Go easy! He ain't just a <u>nobody</u>. His name's Walt. He's a person!" The men emerged from the small tent with a shrouded body on a stretcher. The female officer helped Veronica into the back seat of her cruiser, and the two dogs jumped in. She handed Veronica the black backpack containing the nervous Baxter. As the officer got behind *the wheel, Verna's dreamself approached her daughter and blew gently on her cheeks so to dry her tears. Veronica's head snapped up, eyes searching frantically. "Mom? Izzat you? Mom?" The car drove away, its flickering red and blue lights switched off.*

Verna awakened slowly, rising up through the mists of time and distance. Her surroundings, fusing from fuzzy to clear, focused and became real in the predawn light. As she always experienced when her dreamself returned from Veronica, she had a slight headache. She silently rose from the bed, swallowed an asprirn, and reached for her dream journal to record details of her most recent experience. She wondered what Doctor Hale would say about all of that.

Some say miracles come in all sizes. Perhaps. But miracles are miracles, no matter their size, A miracle is defined as "a highly improbable or extraordinary event or development that brings very welcome consequences; an amazing or wonderful occurrence; an event manifesting considered to be a work of God." The word "miracle" comes from the Latin *miraculum,* meaning "object of wonder." Scholars have traced the word's earliest root origins to early Italic tribes speaking foundations of Latin before 2500 BC, many millennia ago. The ancient word that evolved into "miracle" was "smeiros," meaning "to laugh or to smile."

It was on a Sunday afternoon. A big miracle wrapped in three parts happened to Norman and Verna that day. They were featured as special music in the morning services of "Living Waters of Christ" church in Redding, California and presented an afternoon concert there, well attended and well received. Now they were traveling south on I-5, headed for Sacramento where they were booked for two shows in an elementary school the next day. Serendipitously, the minister of "Living Waters," Reverend Mark Cummings, preached that Sunday morning on expecting miracles. He built his message on Hebrews 11:1. "Now faith is the substance of things hoped for, the evidence of things not seen."

"All of you believe God is real. You believe in the *essence* of God, the *existence* of God, or you probably wouldn't be in this church today," Reverend Cummings said. "You may believe in the *trueness* of God-as-Spirit as opposed to an anthropoidal elderly, long-white-haired, long-white-bearded man sitting on his throne floating somewhere up there in the sky as he studies a huge book that lists those who have been naughty or nice – a figure likened unto Santa Claus in that regard. John's Gospel records Jesus as defining God as a spirit, and those who worship Him must worship Him in spirit. So, yes, there undoubtedly is no question all of us in this room believe in the omnipresent *Spirit of God.* As the Psalmist sang, 'Where can I go from your spirit? Or where can I flee from your presence? If I ascend to heaven, you are there. If I make my bed in Sheol, behold, you are there.' Paul tells us God does not dwell in temples made with hands. The prophet Jeremiah wrote 'Do not I fill heaven and earth?, saith the

Lord.' I could quote Scripture all day about the *realness* of God and His Spirit within, among, and around us all always. We *feel* God. We know *of* Him. We *believe* in His *realness*."

"But do you believe *Him*?" he continued. "Not His Spirit, but *Him*. There's a difference in believing God is real, believing in His *Spirit*, and believing in *Him*, giving Him credit for His Word and His Works. Believing God, *trusting* Him to care for you, *knowing* He will, is called faith. It has been said that faith is expecting from God something that is beyond expectation, It is the confidence that what we hope for will actually happen. Such confidence is assurance about things we cannot yet see, things that have not yet manifested in the physical. Faith is trusting, expecting that God will meet our needs, whatever they may be, and faith manifests miracles. God does things beyond the scope of human imagination, and He calls us to prove our faith in Him. 'Prove me now herewith, saith the Lord of hosts, if I will not open you the windows of heaven, and pour you out a blessing.' Hold fast in your faith and expect your miracles for God is faithful unto you."

"Norman? Something's wrong. The van is going so slow. Feels like we're barely moving." Verna roused up from a doze in the passenger seat.

"Yeah, something is wrong all right. I'm going to get off at the very next exit I see. We gotta get to a repair shop someplace. We started losing power on a slight rise, and now, no matter what I do, we're barely crawling along at fifteen miles an hour. We're on the shoulder, so the freeway traffic is going past us. Good thing we're on flat roadway right now, 'cause I don't think we could climb even the gentlest grade."

Norman's expression was grave as he carefully steered along the bumpy road shoulder. There was an exit coming up: Orland, California – 1 mile. He guided the van through the long, sloping, gently-curving-to-the-right exit ramp, a car behind him honking furiously at his slow pace. The exit ended in a "T." There was an automotive repair garage on the right side of the highway beyond the intersection. It was located amongst a stand of trees, unseen from the interstate nor advertised by billboard, coming into sight at the end of the exit ramp. A weathered sign featuring a grinning horse's face identified it as "Allen's Car & Truck Repair – If We Can't Fix It We'll Get You A Horse." And it was situated at the end of the very next exit Norman saw. That was the first part of the miracle. *The substance of things hoped for…things not seen.*

The highway was clear, so Norman didn't hesitate at the stop sign for fear the van might not go again if it stopped. He turned right and then rolled into the garage's parking lot and to a service bay. The garage was open. On a Sunday afternoon. In the rural hinterlands of northern California, 100 miles from Sacramento. That was the second part of the miracle.

Norman opened the driver's door and stepped out as a mechanic wearing a light blue striped shirt and blue uniform pants appeared. "Hi, there. How you folks doin?" He surveyed the situation. "Your hoss there throw a shoe or sump'n?" His good-natured face crinkled into a smile.

"Well, it just got to going slower and slower all of a sudden. No power hardly. Just all of a sudden. About two miles back. Had to drive on the shoulder of the freeway. Good thing that exit ramp sloped downhill. We just sorta coasted in," Norman replied. "I'm surprised you're open on a Sunday afternoon, but I'm really glad you are."

"Yeah, catchin' up on some work. Got a pickup on tha rack what's suppos'd ta be finished firs' thing inna mornin'. Suppos'd ta've been done Friday, but a Orland *po*-lice car's water pump went out, an' we had ta drive special ta Sacramento ta get one 'cause 'at *po*-lice car's more important than ol' Fred's truck. Orland's only got two of 'em *po*-lice cars, an' was purty important we git t'other'n runnin' agin. So's me an' ma brother, Pete, in 'ere, we opened up tha shop today so's we kin git tha truck finished. Name's John." He extended his hand.

"Norman," shaking John's hand. "So this is your shop?"

"Yeah. Well, me an' Pete's. Was ma dad's originally. Me an' Pete took it over when he got too ol' an' sick ta work. Thought 'bout changin' 'er name ta 'Me an' Pete's,' but left tha ol' name on 'er. Don' wanna go changin' nothin' whut's not broke, ya know. Let's take a look atcher van here an' see whut's goin' on. Losin' power sudden like 'at might be sump'n like a converter gone out."

"A converter?"

"Yeah. A catalytic converter. If'n it is, we'd have ta go inta Sacamento ta git one, an' today's Sunday so won't no part stores be open. Ya'd have ta stay aroun' here tha night."

"Is there a motel close by/"

"Closes' one's 'bout fifteen, twenty mile down tha road 'round Willows. Ya wouldn't wanna drive 'er 'at fur. Might find ya a place some'eres 'round here ya could stay tha night. Hell, if'n it comes to it, we'd putchu inna bay an' lock down tha doors fer tha night. Won't nobody bother ya. But let's take a look at 'er first, though. They's a picnic table yonder in them trees, or ya kin wait inside inf'n ya wants ta, but ain't much of a waitin' room. Couple-a foldin' chairs an' a vendin' machine. Hey, Pete! Let's get this'un up onna rack!"

Whenever they were on a road trip, Verna always packed food and drinks in an ice chest they carried. She would replenish the chest with ice, sandwiches, cookies, and sodas from a convenience store every morning before they began driving for the day. It was a prudent holdover from those long ago "Welfare Days" when she packed peanut-butter-and-jelly sandwiches and iced lemonade in Mason jars for her two young daughters whenever they had to go to doctor or social worker appointments. Now she and Norman carried the chest between them to the picnic table shaded by magnificent ash and oak trees.

As they sat and unwrapped sandwiches, Verna asked, "What did he say?"

"Well, John doesn't know yet. But he said it sounds like it could be the catalytic converter gone bad. If it is, he'll have to go into Sacramento tomorrow or order one. So we might be here at least another day, maybe two. I'll have to call the school tomorrow and cancel. I may have to call the motel in Sacramento and cancel our reservation for tonight." His face fell. The StorySingers had a reputation for punctuality, were never late, and had never missed a performance.

"Where will we stay, Norman? And can we afford this? Sounds expensive." Verna, crestfallen, searched her husband's face. They traveled strictly on cash. And faith. They had no credit card for a road emergency this size.

"Well…the nearest motel is too far away. John said maybe he could find a place we could stay tonight if we have to. He also said, if it comes to it, we could sleep in our van inside a service bay because the doors will be locked down. He said no one wouold bother us. About the repair, we have the cash from our last three appearances, so we may be able to swing it okay. We have some money in savings in Seattle. If there's a branch of our bank anywhere close by, maybe John will take us to it if we need to get money out."

They sat in silence for awhile as they ate their sandwiches. Then…

"Verna, you remember those meditation chants they sing at The Way in Seattle? The ones Reverend Richard taught the congregation before he left? This would be a good time to sing them as our prayer."

They held hands across the table and softly sang.

God takes good care of me. No matter where I go or be. God takes good care of me.

Miracles are happening, yes, miracles are happening, yes, miracles are happening to me. My heart is now open. My mind is receptive. And miracles are happening to me. Right now!

And so they sat in the shade, caressed by a gentle breeze and the songs of birds in the trees surrounding them. They sat in faith, trusting God to take good care of them. They sat, expecting a miracle.

Time passed.

"By dang, it's a miracle, fer shore!" John, whose smile split his face, walked toward them carrying a somewhat charred catalytic converter. "This 'ere's yer converter. She uz done fer, all right, all clogged up an' beginnin' ta heat up sump'n fierce. Butcha'd never believe what happent."

"What, John? What is it?" Norman asked.

"Well, yer van's gotta special kinda converter. Looka here." John placed the now-useless converter on the picnic table. "See? She's a unique 'un, all right. Got two pipes in an' one pipe out 'nstead-a jus' one pipe in an' one pipe out. We'da had ta git one from Sacramento fer shore."

"Don't you still have to?"

"Naw. Ya ain't gonna believe it, but I had this 'un. 'Bout a month ago this feller comes in with a fairly new car what needs a converter jus' like this 'un. So I gets one from Sacramento, an' I'm fixin' ta put 'er on when we finds out his ol' converter's still unner warranty. So, by dang, he says ta go 'head an' order 'im one from tha dealership instead. Says he don' wanna pay fer one if'n he kin git one unner warranty. So's I says 'ok,' an' put 'er up onna shelf. I figgered some'un'd come along off tha I-5 what needs 'er, an' there she'd be a-waitin'. An' here y'are, by golly, an' I happen ta be here onna Sunday. If'n I had'n-a kept 'er, ya'd been a-hurtin' 'cause cain't fin' onena these in no part store nor shop fer at leas' a hunnert mile all aroun,' an' it bein' Sunday an' all, ya know. So ya gotcha a new converter. 'Cause it bein' tha Lord's day an' bein' it's special 'cause I'se open, I'll only charge ya my price fer 'er an' fer labor, which'll be two hunnert an' fifty. Yer all ready ta get back onna road again."

The Love Offering for The StorySingers' concert plus their stipend for special music at "Living Waters of Christ" was $250.00, the exact amount John charged. Norman and Verna got back on the road again and arrived at their Sacramento motel before nightfall.

That was the third part of the miracle.

"Wow," Norman exclaimed as they merged once more into southbound freeway traffic, "Reverend Cummings said in his sermon this morning that God does things beyond the scope of human imagination."

"He does, indeed. Oh, He does. Oh, Norman, what a miracle you are to me! What a miracle we are together!"

Verna and Norman personified perfectly that archaic word "smeiros" as they laughed and smiled at their "object of wonder," their true miracle. In their black van, front and rear bumpers exhorting everyone to EXPECT A MIRACLE, they drove south as they sang loudly and joyfully, "God takes good care of me. No matter where I go or be. God takes good care of me. Miracles are happening, yes, miracles are happening, yes, miracles are happening to me. My heart is now open. My mind is receptive. And miracles are happening to me. Right now!"

Verna reflected once more upon moments building upon moments and the miracles within them. What were the odds that their van's catalytic converter – a unique one, at that – would fail on a Sunday afternoon while driving on Interstate 5 through rural northern California, there would be an auto repair shop at the end of the next exit, it would be open, and there would be the exact new catalytic converter needed waiting for them? *Waiting for them!* The odds were past astronomical, beyond the scope of human imagination as Reverend Cummings mentioned. It was unbelievable. Good words to describe it were implausible, improbable, and impossible. Yet…it happened. Yet…It was real. Yes…It was a miracle. *God takes good care of me. No matter where I go or be. God takes good care of me. Yes…yes, He does…Thank You, Father…Thank You so much!*

Verna and Norman experienced many "miracles on the road" as they crossed the United States performing in myriad venues. Just as they never forgot the "Harvey Field Corn Roast and Fly In," they never forgot "the miracle of the catalytic converter." As the marvel of their meeting on Sunday, March 27, 1987 became a touchstone for them, so, too, did this one. If miracles do indeed come in sizes, this was a huge one!

A DAY OF VOWS, MIRACLES, AND REJOICING

The day was mild, a perfect Arizona clear wintry day – Monday, December 31, 1990. The weather report promised another just like this one tomorrow, a good day to have a wedding, January 1, 1991. June is the traditional month for weddings, but this ceremony was scheduled on the first day of the new year, a symbolic nod to auspicious new beginnings. Norman and Verna were settled inside a luxurious hotel suite, courtesy of Arlene and Robert, Verna's mother and step-father, who came from Orlando for Susanna's ceremony.

Verna basked in the suite's posh surroundings. She and Norman had traveled, performing all the way, from cold, wet Seattle, to warm, dry Tucson. This was their longest tour to date. Since 1987, they had "wet their toes in Entertainment's Waters" via regional week-end and weeks-long tours throughout Washington State, Oregon, and northern California, but this one…this one was a truly special tour as it would bring Verna and Susanna face-to-face once more. This tour was already memorable as the "Miracle of the Catalytic Converter," and *this* tour would expand their repute nationwide – a *10-month* tour!

As the reputation of the The StorySingers grew, calls came in constantly for bookings, especially in churches. In some instances, they provided the entire Sunday morning service as well as a concert in the afternoon or evening. There were other venues as well – school assemblies, performance centers, festivals, custom-designed shows for holidays, events, and special concerns such as their Substance Abuse Show for elementary schools; somehow all of it meshed together perfectly. In both religious and secular venues, The StorySingers became known as "inspirational entertainers." It was exhilarating for both Norman and Verna, yet they kept themselves grounded in faith. Verna, as was her custom since childhood, often referred to her Bible for guidance. Now, in her new life with Norman as an entertainer, one of her favorite verses was Isaiah 43:19, "Behold, I do a new thing; now it shall spring forth; shall ye not know it? I will even make a way in the wilderness, and rivers in the desert." Truthfully, both Verna's and Norman's new lives *had* sprung forth, and they knew it. They also knew God made a way for them in their wilderness, for their new life was indeed an uncharted wilderness as they set forth in faith to cross the continent, entertaining as they went.

Norman wrote a storysong entitled "The Linden Tree."

There's a Wonderland called Once Upon a Time,
A Place where the mind soars free.
Some say it dims through passing time:
Find it again at the Linden Tree.

In the Wonderland called Once Upon a Time,
A Place where the mind soars free,
There's a spot where clocks never measure Time,
And on that spot grows the Linden Tree.

And now it grows, that Linden Tree,
Straight and tall it stands,
Growing dreams for you and me...
The dreams you dream in Wonderland!

The StorySingers now closed church concerts with "The Linden Tree" and offered a seedling to be planted on the church grounds. Doing so made this tour all the more satisfying and meaningful. Hopefully, a church would either plant its seedling in its meditation garden or, if it didn't have one, create such a space around the seedling – a space where "the mind soars free." Distribution of seedlings was a tribute to Norman's personal "meditation garden" where he sat in silence and felt Verna's powerful energy coming his way on Sunday, March 27, 1987. Currently, the flat of baby trees they brought with them was sitting under the van in the shade. Norman periodically went outside to the hotel's parking lot to spritz them and inspect for signs of wilting. So far, they had all endured the journey well.

"Mama, do you need your dress pressed? I'm rather good at ironing, you know." Verna smiled at her mother who had just knocked on the hotel suite's door.

"Well, now, that's a good idea. I'll bring it by later." Arlene smiled, then had a thought. "I'm wondering if I should wait to change into it tomorrow when we get to Old Tucson, so it won't get wrinkled wearing it in the car." She beamed at her daughter. "What do you think?"

Verna looked lovingly at her mother, every inch the matriarch. Hair gone gray, but stylishly colored, she still bore a youthful appearance.

She looks...content...happily content...and more beautiful than ever...it's good that Robert came into her life so soon after Daddy's death...I wonder how she feels being Mrs. Robert Carrolton now instead of Mrs. Frank Davidson...oh, well, none of my business, anyway...and Robert is a nice man...still getting used to him as a step-father, though.

"Well...the setting at Old Tucson is lovely for a wedding, but I'm not real certain what kind of facilities there will be for ladies. Best to dress here in the hotel and be all set when we arrive." Arlene's dress, elegant brocade in a soft mauve, suited her perfectly. As always she'd ordered it from a catalog, then had it altered by a seamstress for a flawless fit. She adored catalogs, and went "armchair shopping" every day.

"What's Norman doing?" Arlene glanced around the room and noted his absence.

"Watering the trees," replied Verna, absently.

"Trees! Why? The hotel waters its own trees, I'm sure!"

"Not the hotel's landscaping, Mama," Verna chuckled, "the seedling trees we're bringing with us on this tour. They're under the van in the shade. He takes care of them. I believe he even talks to them."...smile..."Sit down, Mama." She indicated the only upholstered chair.

The two women visited, catching each other up. Both prolific letter writers, they were up to date with the happenings in each other's lives, but it was so good to talk live; they couldn't get enough.

"Have you seen Susanna?" Arlene's brows arched questioningly.

"Only at the bridesmaids' luncheon yesterday." Verna's face fell at the memory. Anne Marie preferred that Verna have no part in the wedding preparations, but Susanna insisted, so there they were. Not close enough at the table to actually talk, but at least Verna was there and gloried in seeing her daughter. Now she sighed heavily that she couldn't fill her role as mother of the bride.

"Isn't she lovely, though?" Arlene saw that her question upset her daughter and hastened on. "Her hair is all the way down her back. I wonder if she'll have it styled in an upsweep for the ceremony or let it be loose?"

"You know Susanna. Her hair is always going to be her own decision," laughed Verna. "I met Chase and his parents. They are so nice. And he is a very handsome young man." Verna smiled at the memory of first meeting her future son-in-law. "Such lovely manners. Proud of his heritage. His ancestry is of the Kentucky Boones, he said, which included Daniel. He's a teacher here in Tucson, you know."

Arlene nodded. "Yes. I think it's a great match." She smiled softly. "They love each other."

And so the two women chatted, both ignoring the elephant in the room, the fact that Verna was no longer legally Susanna's mother.

"Have you ever heard from Veronica?" Arlene asked. Then immediately regretted the asking. No one had had any word from Susanna's older sister since the day she disappeared. Some speculated she was dead. Surprisingly, though, Verna's face remained pleasant, not stricken with sadness.

"Well...not exactly."

Now Arlene's eyebrows shot up into her hairline. "Not exactly? You either have or you haven't. Nobody's heard from her. What on earth do you mean?"

Verna took a deep steadying breath. "No, I haven't *heard* from her. But... occasionally I *dream* of her. In fact, I think sometimes I find her...somehow... when I'm dreaming. I can't talk to her, or her to me, but in my dreams I see her. Sometimes she's walking along a highway with a big dog. Sometimes at a campfire with...with a...friend. Sometimes in a city. Once I saw her cooking breakfast in a beautiful kitchen. Yellow gingham curtains, yellow cookie jar made like an upright yellow butter pat, yellow napkin holder, table set with white placemats and dishes with yellow sunflowers on them. She was wearing a pink bathrobe, had a towel around wet hair, and making eggs over easy." Verna smiled to herself at the memory. There were others. Veronica in a hospital corridor, running. Veronica in a police station apparently being booked. Veronica on a blanket at the beach, drinking beer. She decided to not mention those dreams to her mother.

"So, no, I've not *heard* from her, but I feel that I have *visited* her and she is okay." Arlene's jaw dropped, and, for a moment, wondered if her daughter, in her sadness, had taken leave of her senses.

Norman entered the room, spritzer bottle in hand. "Well, the seedlings seem to be okay." He noticed Arlene. "Oh. Hello, there, Arlene. Don't you look fine!" He set the spritzer bottle down and hugged his mother-in-law.

"Why, thank you, Norman. I was just going. Tomorrow is the big day. Our baby is getting married!" She glanced at Verna with a smile.

"And she is a beautiful bride. How could she not be with such a beautiful mother and grandmother?" Norman winked.

As they drove to Old Tucson the next day, Verna remembered the first time she'd seen the place. A patient at Mesquite Valley Mental Hospital, she had danced in the rain with her roommate, Sue, when a select group of patients went on a supervised "outing." She chuckled to herself at the memory. *My how time flies...* Norman looked at her inquiringly, and Verna told him briefly about that day. He knew of her experience as a catatonic patient in Mesquite Valley, but he'd not heard about her and her roommate dancing in a rainstorm. He laughed aloud.

"The two of you...actually...danced?"

"Oh, yeah. We did the twist, we did the bump, we did the cha cha, and we boogied on down!" Verna laughed at the memory.

Norman said, "Back then could you have ever dreamed of this day? Your youngest daughter's wedding being held at Old Tucson? And you getting to be here?" He glanced sideways at his wife.

"Never. Not in a million years. Just think of all the miracles that had to happen to make this day possible. One was my friend, Janice, who helped relay the letters between me and Susanna, sustaining the relationship. You, chief among them. You got us here by booking this tour and managing our budget so we'd have traveling money." Verna looked lovingly at her husband. "You, my dear, are a wonder."

The wedding ceremony was to be held outside, timed to be at sunset, when the colors would light up the sky and reflect off the white face of the faux chapel, actually only a facade. The reception would be inside a real building. The Old Tucson campus was a movie set, so the chapel frontage had been many things in its movie lifetime: a church, a fortress, a warehouse. Today it was the backdrop for Susanna's and Chase's open air wedding. When the event was being planned, its front was white stucco. But, due to a recent renovation for an upcoming film, it now was colored a variety of tans, umbers, and brief streaks of brown. The bride had *not* been happy, but there was nothing to be done about it.

The chapel unit was at one end of a string of false building fronts next to a wooden sidewalk stretching down the dirt street, a saloon at the other end. If the string of buildings were on a stage, the chapel would be at the far left, and the saloon would be at the far right as seen from the audience. A portable latticed archway festooned with artificial Baby's Breath flowers mixed with mock multi-colored carnations, compliments of Old Tucson Nuptials, stood on the sidewalk in front of the chapel door and defined the ceremony's staging area. The minister stood underneath the arch. To his right a musician dressed in a long black coat, red shirt, blue jeans, rhinestone-studded boots, and a black ten-gallon hat with a red hatband, stood at a synthesizer, his "organ," playing and singing his arrangement of "Cowboy Wedding Song" by Clint Eastwood. The synthesizer was plugged into a movie-sized sound system, so everyone present could hear very well. Four groomsmen in pale blue tuxedos and royal blue cummerbunds stood in place. A white paper wedding runner stretched about 30 feet from the edge of the sidewalk into the street and delineated the "aisle" down which the bride would walk to the "altar." One hundred metal folding chairs faced the archway, fifty chairs on each side of the paper runner. Almost every chair was occupied. People were ready for a wedding. There was much convivial chatter, most of it competing with Clint's song. It was somewhat surreal.

A strengthening desert breeze sprang up, playfully skittering a few tumbleweeds around, tousling people's hair, and ruffling lacy hats. Those in charge of preparations attempted to keep the white paper wedding runner firmly on the sand and gravel, but wafts of wind kept lifting the white paper, so children were sent to gather rocks to hold it down. The kids were as delighted as if they were on a treasure hunt. "Here! I got a big'un!" "Over here! I got one bigger!" A tiny girl in bouffant blue gathered pebbles in the pinafore of her dress, and scattered them artistically over the paper as she flung them like rose petals.

Suddenly a bugle blast, whinnies, hoofbeats, the rattle of wheels, and a "Hi yah, get up there!" were heard from the far right end of the line of building fronts.

People turned to look as, in a true Old Tucson style "cloud-of-dust-rocks-flying-bugle-blowing entrance," the bride arrived in an authentic Old West stagecoach drawn by four white, rather excited, horses. It was followed by a two-horse team pulling a wooden wagon in which bounced four bridesmaids, holding to the sides for dear life. The stagecoach driver wore a white western rancher's suit with a bolo tie featuring a big turquoise clasp, and a white Stetson hat. The bugle-blowing wrangler, wearing traditional denim jeans, buckskin chaps, western boots, leather vest, brown plaid shirt with bolo tie adorned with a gold horseshoe, and a worn brown felt cowboy hat with a jaunty feather in the snakeskin hatband, sat next to him on the driver's bench. He was holding on to his hat with one hand, trying to keep his bugle steady with the other, bouncing with every jarring jolt of the coach, and attempting to play a bugle royal entrance fanfare. But, because of the carriage's swaying and jouncing, it merely came out in short, staccato, brass burps. *Wah, wah..boosh...wah..bllth..wonnk...bffft..wannh...* The bride's veil, in a long flutter of white net adorned with tiny white Irish crocheted roses, streamed from the coach's window like a comet's fluttering tail or a long strip of extra-wide toilet paper stuck to someone's shoe inside the coach. Those roses on that veil, however, were Verna's only donation to the wedding, and she felt a surge of righteous pride at sight of them. "Whoa there, now," said the driver as he pulled back on the reins, and, amid snorting, pawing, and a final, weak, flat horn blow...*blaaat*...the coach stopped at the end of the rock-weighted white runner. The bridesmaids' wagon creaked to a stop behind it. Verna marveled at the theatrics of it all, especially the driver's precision of stopping the coach so its side door was perfectly aligned with the wind-ruffled white paper runner, now struggling like a live thing attempting to free itself from its pebbled imprisonment and sail away on the breeze like the majestic banner it was meant to be.

The organist played "She'll be Comin' 'Round the Mountain" at the bugle's first blast, and the apparition of stagecoach, horses, dust, streaming white veil, and female-filled wagon appeared around the side of Ward's Saloon & Trading Post at the far end of the movie set's street; then he segued into the familiar sedate Wedding March as the stagecoach and wagon stopped. All rock-gathering children had been dusted off and placed back in seats where they belonged. Robert, Arlene, Norman, and Verna, all wearing expectant and happy expressions, sat in the second row from the front on the bride's side, each adorned with their respective corsage or boutonniere.

The desert breeze increased in velocity and became a swooshing wind, whirling dust in its blowing. The horses snorted and sneezed as the dust tickled their nostrils. The stagecoach driver, holding onto his hat with one hand and the reins in the other, kept saying "Whoa, now. Easy there," as he did his best to keep the stagecoach steady in place. Women wearing hats held onto them with one hand. Men held their hats on with one hand and their ties down with the other. The white paper wedding runner, ignoring the various rocks placed along its length, snapped and tore at its edges in its wild desire to escape the ground and swirl away like an air-borne snake. The bugling wrangler's hat blew off as he climbed down from his seat to open the coach door for the party inside.

He opened the door and tipped an imaginary hat to the flower girl, first out of the coach, traditional basket on her arm. The wind immediately sent all the petals flying, dancing and twirling merrily in the air. In vain the little girl grasped for them, and her sweet face puckered into a frown. Next out was the ring bearer in his miniature tux, clutching the white satin heart-shaped pillow firmly with both hands. He held it to his chest protectively as he jumped out of the coach. Patrick, handsomely dressed in a rented black tux, exited next, his hair immediately disheveled in the wind. Gallantly, he extended a hand to assist Susanna down. A strong gust hit the side of the coach momentarily rocking it, startling the horses and causing them to whinny and stomp with alarm. "Whoa, now. Easy there." Susanna lost her footing, fell into her father's arms, and they both laughed.

The organist played the wedding march up tempo. The little flower girl started her march up the shredding aisle, held her empty basket, and mimed throwing rose petals while blowing kisses at the crowd. The little ring bearer kept his head down and placed his feet carefully on the flapping white paper as if to do so would tame it into submission and keep it from flying away all together.

Grit and sand blew into Verna's eyes, and she wiped them. Her mother turned her head away from the direction of the wind and swiped at her eyes as well. Robert had Frank's old 35 mm camera around his neck and was taking pictures with every step the wedding party took. The bridesmaids in matching royal blue chiffon, a bit wobbly after their bouncing ride, paraded along, clutching their bouquets of pink roses in one hand, holding their miniature veils on their heads with the other.

Then the bride and her father stepped onto the paper runner, and everyone stood in the traditional salute to the bride. Verna's breath caught in her throat at the vision. Susanna, holding her bouquet of pink Sweetheart Roses cascading down the front of her gown, long brown silken hair flowing, was radiant in bouffant white satin, overlaid with lace, encrusted with seed pearls and small crystals. They glittered and sparkled in the light from the setting sun. Her shoes, ivory silk pumps, were similarly encrusted, bringing thoughts of Cinderella to Verna's mind. Tears of joy for her daughter threatened, along with tears of loss and anger at Patrick. She tamped the myriad emotions down as the wedding proceeded.

The minister asked, "Who gives this woman to be wed to this man?" Patrick answered, "Her family and I do." Chase, in a white tuxedo, stepped forward and took Susanna's hand as she handed her bouquet to her maid of honor. The little ring bearer stood close by, now hugging the important satin pillow firmly to his narrow chest.

The ceremony swam by for Verna as she was flooded with so many memories. Susanna, hot with measles' fever, swaddled in a towel asking for the story of the Little Engine That Could. Susanna, singing "Ol' Dan Tucker" as she rode on the back of Verna's bicycle in the little passenger seat. Susanna, arm hideously burned in an accident with the iron, shrieking in the doctor's office as the injury was tended. Susanna, carrying Zipper, their black kitten, around on her shoulder. Susanna, in her pillowcase ghost costume at Halloween saying, "Boo. I a ghostie." Now, here she was, towering nearby, a stunning vision of a bride. Verna was a bit breathless with it all.

A late model gray Jeep Cherokee featuring "Storage Solutions" painted in dark maroon on both front doors rolled to a stop about 20 yards away from the ceremonial proceedings. A light-brown-haired young woman dressed in a business suit sat quietly behind the wheel and watched the wedding unfold. She observed the bride and groom walk down the wind-whipped paper aisle, followed by their family members and the rest of the attendees as they strode across the dusty, sand-swirled street and disappeared into a huge building with a banner "Boone Wedding Reception" flapping above its double front doors. She sat silently a few moments. Then she gently opened the driver's door, got out, and calmly walked to the reception.

The reception was held in one of Old Tucson's sound stages, a cavernous building roughly the size of an airplane hangar. Verna didn't get to speak to her daughter until she was in the reception line. Then, they didn't speak. They hugged. Neither dared try to talk for fear of tears. Verna hugged Chase, too, and he whispered in her ear, "Thank you for such a beautiful bride. She takes after you."

Janice and Derek Sawtelle were there, Verna's dear friends in Tucson. *Strange how things go around...Janice and Derek gave me shelter in Nineteen Seventy after Patrick beat me so badly...Janice paid airfare to Orlando then for me, Susanna, and Veronica...they took me in again after Patrick and Anne Marie so deviously adopted Susanna and Veronica away from me when I lived in Orlando, and I came to Tucson to try and get them back...now here we all are again...a strange mix of people, to be sure...an odd merry-go-round of life...*

Verna, Norman, Robert, and Arlene sat with Janice and Derek at one of the big round tables. None of the swirling conversation stuck in Verna's mind. Vaguely she was aware there was a DJ playing the newlyweds' favorite music. Dimly she saw couples dancing. As she sat staring vacantly around at the crowd, she suddenly saw a girl standing in the doorway. No. Not a girl. A young woman. With light brown hair that shone in the overhead lights. Dressed tastefully in a navy blue business suit, stockings, and heels. *...Someone late for the festivities?... Hmmm...She looks familiar...She looks like...she looks...like...she...oh!...oh, my God!* Verna was on her feet running before she even realized she'd stood.

It was Veronica. In the flesh. She was real! Verna put her arms around her eldest daughter and swung her around in a circle. She wanted to shriek with happiness but, throat thick with emotion, no sound would come. It was a

"Prodigal Returned Moment!" It was a miracle! An odd "merry-go-round of life" moment indeed!

"Hi, Mom. How're ya doin'?"

Dimly, Verna was aware there were other people clustering around them, and the decibel level had risen from a hum to a roar. Then she realized she was being hugged from behind. Verna was between both her daughters. She turned so she could see them together. She was reunited with her girls once more! So many years had passed, years of heartache, despair, guilt, and sorrow. Years of beseeching prayers as well as affirming ones. Years of an empty ache only a mother could feel for her lost children. Now, in an instant, those years vaporized like snowflakes on hot asphalt – *poof...*gone! And fragments of Verna's broken heart melded together again.

The room lit up with flashbulbs. Then Chase was at Susanna's side, and his parents followed. Norman appeared, then Patrick and Anne Marie. It made a stunning photo.

The rest of the evening whisked by in shrieks of joy, wedding toasts, dancing, cake, celebration, and reunions. What a night it was, not only for Verna, but also for sisters long parted, for families reunited, for healing of hearts. Finally, revelries came to an end as adrenalin drained away and a tired, peaceful contentment replaced it. The bride and groom left on their honeymoon in their decorated car; Verna and Norman took Veronica to their hotel room. Robert and Arlene, exhausted, bade everyone goodnight and went to their suite.

Norman discreetly left to "tend the seedling trees, get a cuppa coffee in the lounge, and let you girls talk awhile," leaving Verna and Veronica alone.

They sat and gazed at each other. "You're so beautiful," breathed Verna as she gazed into the face she had seen so many times in her dreams. "I have lots of questions, as I'm sure you do, too, but I gotta ask this one first. How come you named your dog Kitty?"

Taken by surprise, Veronica burst out laughing. She was overcome with gales of giggles and couldn't speak for a bit. Then she asked, "How do you know I had a dog named Kitty?" She sipped water from the hotel room glass and sobered somewhat.

Not quite sure how to proceed, Verna said softly, "I dreamed of you. You also had a dog named Lady, a brindle boxer I think, and there was a small black-and-white dog named Baxter."

Abruptly, Veronica turned away and started to cry. Verna went to her, put her arms around her and stroked her hair. "I sort of...visited you...when I was dreaming. You had a denim backpack embroidered with all kinds of designs. You wore a blue bandanna."

"So you *were* there! I thought I imagined it. That time in the woods when I was being chased...and when Walt died..." her voice trailed off.

"And the Christmas he gave you a paperback of 'The Call of the Wild.'" Verna smiled and returned to her chair. She wanted to mention the beautiful yellow kitchen, but decided to not.

Veronica took a deep breath and let it out slowly. "Well...Walt got the big dog when she was just a pup. He also got a small cat. Didn't so much get it on purpose. It just followed him around. The two played together, slept together, were inseparable." She looked almost bashful. "So, whenever he called the cat, he'd say, 'Here Kitty! Here Kitty!' and the dumb pup would come, too. So the puppy thought her name was Kitty." She chuckled a little. "By the time I met him, Kitty was nigh on two hundred pounds, and the cat had long since gone."

Verna made coffee in the little hotel coffeepot and they sipped from plastic cups as they talked. Norman returned quietly, said his "good nights," and slipped into the suite's bedroom and left mother and daughter to their conversation.

Veronica, it turned out, was Marketing Manager for Storage Solutions, a company in Anchorage, Alaska that maintained storage tanks as well as supplying tanks to other companies. Serendipitously, she was in Tucson to investigate tanks made by custom manufacturers and distributors and perhaps recruit them as Storage Solutions clients. The City of Tucson was a client, as Storage Solutions maintained the city's vehicle fleet's gasoline storage tanks, so she also courtesy called upon Tucson's General Services Director. She saw Susanna's wedding announcement in the newspaper so thought to just quietly slip in to the wedding and leave unnoticed. But the sight of her mother and her sister compelled her to complete the reunion, so she went to the soundstage where the reception was. She was now Veronica Brand, married to Don Brand, president of Storage Solutions.

"How did you meet Don?" Verna inquired.

"Well, after Walt died, I decided to hitch up to Skagway 'cause I'd always wanted to see Alaska, and Skagway sounded so, well, romantic. I thought I might pan for gold up there also. I lived a free life as a runaway, Mom. I still do, in a way. That's why I like marketing trips like this one, so I can get away from the office and travel free for awhile. Don understands."

"He sounds like a good man."

"He is. He's a kindred spirit. I met him when I was panning in a little creek running off the Skagway River. He was fly fishing, and we got to talking. He was a painter for Storage Solutions then, He and a crew were in Skagway painting the inside of empty storage tanks. Usually when a storage tank is emptied, it needs maintenance such as cleaning and painting."

"How often?"

"Well, it depends. Water storage tanks usually about every year should be emptied, cleaned, inspected, and painted. Fuel tanks should be inspected on a regular basis, we advise at least every three months, and emptied once a year for maintenance cleaning and painting."

"Sounds like it is a good business."

"It is. Keeps us busy, all right. So Don and I got together. We were really good for each other. Still are. We kinda inspired each other to settle down, so he really worked hard over the years, got promotions. Became crew foreman, then supervisor, then office manager. And, when the owner retired, took over Storage Solutions. We have six crews of ten men each which we send out all over the western Canadian provinces and the western lower forty-eight states. Probably have to hire some more after I get back from this trip. There's a big tank and pipe company in Portland I want to visit on my way back. Portland Tank and Pipe, it's called."

"Why did you never try to get in touch with me, Sweetheart? After you settled down?"

"Oh, Mom, I didn't know how. I was afraid. I knew how much my disappearing probably hurt daddy, Anne Marie, and you. And Susanna. I felt really bad about leaving her. Even Grandmother Davidson, I know I must have hurt her, too. But I couldn't live in that chaos anymore. Even when I was thirteen, when I was that young, I couldn't live with daddy and Anne Marie and Granny anymore. Not in all that yucky tobacco smoke and bickering all the time and Granny always drunk and drooling. I had to get away. And I felt so guilty. I didn't know how to get in touch with you."

"Well, you're here now, and that's what counts."

They sat in silence a moment. Then…

"Did you ever find any?"

"What?"

"Gold. Did you ever find any gold when you were panning?"

"Oh. Yes. Yes, I did. One nugget. I made it into a pendant. See?"

Veronica removed from around her neck a gold nugget embedded in a mother-of-pearl pendant hanging on a gold chain. Inscribed on the back of the pendant were the words "Forever Free!"

"This meant a lot to me. You know how much I love to read and how much I love being free. These are Frederick Douglas' words. He said 'Once you learn to read, you'll be forever free.' Books made me free, especially my favorite 'The Call of the Wild.' Now I'm free from the anguish of not contacting you all those years. I want you to have this."

"Oh, Sweetheart, I couldn't."

"Yes, Mom, you can. Here, please let me."

Veronica placed the necklace around Verna's neck. The transfer completed their reunion, and fissures in both hearts fused, making them whole again.

They sat together for a long time as the night softly slipped away.

The next morning, after sharing an early hearty complimentary breakfast, reunited family members parted once more following huge goodbye hugs, several tear-flavored kisses on tear-streaked cheeks, and repeated "So good to see yous," "God bless yous," and "Keep in touch now, y'hears." Veronica headed west on I-10 as she began her trip back to Alaska. She would take the year-round ferry from Bellingham, WA to Haines, Alaska and then drive on to Anchorage. She liked the ferry ride. It allowed her time to think, to reminisce about her experiences. It had been a most eventful trip for her. She was excited to get home and tell Don all about it. She had so much to share about her reunion with her mother and Susanna. She hoped she would have good news about Portland Tank and Pipe. She would.

Norman placed the flat of baby trees back in the van.

Arlene and Frank took the hotel shuttle to Tucson International for their flight back to Orlando.

How many times I have flown that route, thought Verna as she closed her mother's shuttle door. *Frantically flying away from Tucson to Orlando in Nineteen Seventy to escape Patrick after the divorce...then in Nineteen Seventy Four flying from Orlando back here to try and legally overturn Patrick and Anne Marie's sneaky adoption of the girls...oh, I know those flights well...and what a difference twenty-one years makes...me, a single mother with two small daughters who had to subsist on welfare and taking in ironing...being raped and having a beautiful baby girl...oh, I hope I get to see Chrissy again sometime... then becoming an LPN who became an OR Nurse, and a good one at that...then working as a veterinarian's surgical assistant to being a Teamster shop steward for The Seattle Times to where I am now, an extremely happily married woman and an accomplished musician and entertainer who is traveling the nation entertaining thousands...yeah, Jerry, who would want to hear a fat lady sing?...a lot of people!...hundreds of 'em listen to this lady sing...oh, wow!...what a journey this has been!...what a journey it will be!...thank You, Father...thank You so much...I know You go before me and prepare my way!*

Verna and Norman, he behind the wheel and she in the passenger seat, sat in their black van in the hotel's parking lot. "Oh, what a trip this has been so far," he said. "Who could have imagined?"

"I know. You know, you would have to be me to understand, to *get*, how extraordinary, how miraculous, *all* of this has been...and *is!*...to me. Oh, dear God, Norman, never would I have thought I could be this happy, this complete, this loved."

"Nor I. I love you very much!"

"And I you, dearest man."

"Well, shall we get started? It's El Paso next stop. We've got two school shows tomorrow and three shows for the Sunland Park Mall Winter Festival on Saturday."

"One moment. I want to savor this right now." Verna reached for her travel Bible in the glove compartment. She opened it to Psalm 28:7. "You know, Sweetheart, this verse in Psalms has meant so much to me, especially because of all that's happened and the miracle of meeting you." She read aloud. "The Lord is my strength and my shield; my heart trusted in him, and I am helped. Therefore my heart greatly rejoiceth; and with my song will I praise him."

Verna closed her Bible, reached over, and took Norman's hand.

"Oh, my darling Norman, my heart does so greatly rejoiceth."

"Rejoice always!" – 1 Thessalonians 5:16

EPILOGUE

The year was 1993. Verna and Norman were offered a position as Music Ministers in a Florida church; they accepted, moved to Melbourne, FL, and "came off the road." Though comfortable with their decision, it took time to adapt to their new status, no longer appearing in schools, malls, and various events. Their "StorySingers" personas were packed away with puppets, props, and their soft-sculptured fireplace. *I'll be forever adapting,* thought Verna, *I miss being a StorySinger.*

Verna answered the phone in their new Florida home. It was Susanna. She and Chase, now proud parents of a 2-month-old baby girl, Tallie, both taught in the Tucson public school system. She was at home, enjoying the last 3 weeks of the February 1993 federal Family and Medical Leave Act. Tallie was born in March, so the FMLA was passed just in time for Susanna to take advantage of the 12 weeks the law allowed for her job absence. Susanna, now a mother, felt an urgency for Verna to locate Chrissy.

"Mom? Listen. You just gotta find her! I mean, well, you've got me and Ronnie back, so you need to find our little sister. And I want Tallie to know her aunt. So you gotta find her. You just gotta." There was pleading in her voice.

Verna sighed. Ever since the wedding almost two-and-a-half years ago, Susanna had been going on about this. Verna had mixed feelings, an endless litany of "What ifs?" repeated itself in her mind – What if "Chrissy" was never told she was adopted? What if she was orphaned by her adopted parents? What if she wants nothing to do with me? What if she is a dreadful human being? What if, God forbid, she's *dead?* What if?...what if?...what if?

"Mom? Mom? You there?" Susanna's voice was impatient. Verna could hear the baby babbling in the background.

"Yes, Honey, I'm here. I just don't know if it's a wise move. I mean…heck… there are so many things to think about. I want to do what's best here, y'know?"

"Mom, what's best is you find my baby sister. I want to know all about her. I want to talk to her. I want to…hug her." A shriek ensued in the background, followed by wails. "I gotta go. The puppy just barked at the baby and startled her. Find her, Mom. Find my sister!" *…click…*

The phone rang again.
"Hello? Verna speaking."

"Hi, Mom."

"Veronica! Sweetheart! How nice it is to get to talk to you on the phone now. Where are you?"

"In Anchorage. Actually, I'm calling from the office, so kinda got to make this short. SuSu called me yesterday and wanted me to be sure and call you."

"Susanna did?"

"Yeah."

"She just called me awhile ago. I bet I know what it's about. She wants you to tell me to find Chrissy, doesn't she?"

"Well, yeah, that's it. But, you know, Mom, she's right. We all need some kind of closure on this. Me, you, Susanna. Even Chrissy. You know, she might be looking for you."

"I understand. You are aware, of course, that her name might not be Chrissy at all. That was just some kind of thought that passed through my mind back then."

"I know, Mom. We've talked about that. But when SuSu and I were kids, we blessed our little sister, Chrissy, in our prayers every night. Remember?"

"Oh, of course I do, Sweetheart. All too well. Like I told Susanna, I want to do what's best here. Let me think some more about it."

"Well, don't think too much longer, Mom. Make an effort, at least. Our family was split apart years ago, and we need to be whole again if we can be. I know. I have my share of blame for running away like I did. I'm sorry for my part in breaking us all up, but at least you and me and SuSu are connected again. That's important. And I sure hope we can connect with my baby sister also, whatever her name is. Talk to Norman about it."

"I will, Sweetheart."

"Good. Gotta go. Great talking with you. Don sends his love and a hug."

"Hug him back for me. Bye. Love you."

"Love you, too, Mom. Bye." *...click...*

"Well, Honey, God has guided us this far. I think you just need to pray about it, put your faith in His guidance, and go for it."

"Oh, Norman, I have prayed about it. So much. But I'm afraid."

"I know you are. But, you know, it's like the fears we faced when we were touring, going out there in the world without knowing what we were going to run into. Like the time of the catalytic converter, remember? That was scary, but all we could do was just go forward in faith. And look how that turned out. Look at how everything turned out. The fear is really only fear of the unknown. I mean, that repair shop was right there waiting for us at the end of the exit, and so was the converter we needed. But we didn't know it. That's what caused our fear, my fear. The unknown. So you'll never know unless you try. You'll always be afraid of the unknown."

"You're right, dearest man. I will call."

"Children's Home Society, Mrs. Blankenship speaking." For a moment, Verna froze. She didn't quite know how to begin. The voice spoke again. "Hello? Hello?"

"Hi, there, uh, Mrs. Blankenship. My name is Verna Davidson. You have me in your records as Verna Williams. May I speak with Mrs. Dixon?" She held her breath, unaware she was doing so.

"Oh. Yes. Mrs. Dixon."—pause—"Um, I am so sorry to have to tell you, but she passed away. About a year and a half ago. I'd be happy to help you, though. What do you need?"

Sadness whooshed through Verna like a cold wind, chilling her blood, shivering her spine, taking her breath. She never expected to hear *this!* She had always thought of Mrs. Dixon as solid, real, and as eternal as a boulder on a mountain. Mrs. Dixon had always been there for her. The cheerful, chubby, always impeccably attired, personification of Mrs. Santa Claus – *that* Mrs. Dixon! Gone? How could she be *gone?*

"Oh…uh…well, I'm a birth mother, you see. Mrs. Dixon was my…uh… social worker in Nineteen Seventy One when I gave my baby up for adoption. I just…just wanted to…to talk with her."

"I see, "replied the calm voice. "Let's make an appointment, shall we?"

Weeks passed. The search didn't take as long as Verna expected. The reunion was scheduled for the coming Saturday. She couldn't sleep. She couldn't do much of anything but pace. When she did remain still, Norman held her, infusing her with his love. Through his hugs, Verna knew that, no matter what happened, she would always be loved.

Past images flitted across her memory's screen…*a Labor and Delivery Nurse just coming on shift mistakenly placed the newborn girl on Verna's chest, unaware the plan was for the baby to go straight to the nursery so it would be easier for Verna to give her up if she didn't see her. In the brief moment mother and infant looked in each other's eyes, there was an instant, transcendental heart connection. "I'm Chrissy," the thought flowed into Verna.. "I'm Verna Louise. I'm your mother," communicated Verna. The nurse removed the newborn and murmured apologies that she hadn't known about the plan.*

Then Verna's memory changed to that terrible day she signed the legal adoption documents. Vernoica in overwhelming pain from an abscessed tooth, walked along with her and Susanna to the Children's Home Society as they prayed to find a dentist. Miraculously, they found one along the way, a dentist whose practice was in his home. Verna left Veronica in his care while she, carrying Susanna, hurried the rest of the way for her appointment with an attorney and Mrs. Dixon.

Verna saw her baby daughter for the second and last time that day. She was given the unexpected opportunity to hold her, feed her a bottle, and change her. She marveled then at "Chrissy's" perfection. It was heartbreaking to sign the documents. Tears rose at the memory, and her throat tightened. *What will she be like now?*

Saturday dawned clear and bright. The day of all days had arrived! The small red car Verna had been told to expect turned into her driveway, and she ran to meet it. All she knew about her daughter was that she'd been adopted by a family named Carson and currently worked in a gift shop at Disney World.

A tall, lovely young woman with dishwater blonde hair and wearing sunglasses emerged from the car. Verna threw her arms around her, and the lovely young woman removed her dark glasses as she hugged her mother. Verna saw her own hazel green eyes looking back at her.

From an infinite, mystical, mist of two souls' swirling spheres, those thoughts transferred telepathically years ago now coalesced, formed themselves into words, and the young woman spoke.

"I'm Chrissy."

"I'm Verna Louise. I'm your mother."

"Actually, Christina Carson. But everybody calls me Chrissy."

"Come inside, my dear. We have so much to talk about."

The circle, finally complete, was now unbroken.

"Will the circle be unbroken, by and by, Lord, by and by?
Now the family is parted; will it be complete one day?"

Ada R. Habershon, 1907

THE STORYSINGERS
1987 – 1993

(Promotional Photograph taken by the late Clarice Keegan)

The StorySingers have aptly been called "Memory Makers," "Caretakers of Wonder," and "Troubadours of God." – From a promotional poster

ABOUT THE AUTHOR

Vashti Ataya, a multi-talented guitarist, songwriter, storyteller, and author, experienced an exciting, diverse childhood as she was born an only child into a military family. Living in Panama, Germany, and rural Oklahoma afforded her wide-ranging opportunities to soak in unique cultures and customs as her parents toured Europe and Central America while deployed in those duty stations. Throughout her formative years, her worldview was seasoned with the tolerance of acceptance of new, perhaps strange, traditions and lifestyles. Her first book, "MEMORIES, Chronicles of a Grateful Life," recounts some of those past noteworthy experiences, such as "Grandma Josie's Dishes," "The Belcher House Fire," and "The Wedding." Available on Amazon.com as well as Barnes & Noble.com, "MEMORIES" provides an authentic foundation for this Autobiographical Fiction Series.

Vashti is a genuine, loving soul, and her genuineness is peppered throughout her writing, flavoring it with fresh tangs and tastes for the reader's eye. She is excited about her 5-book OVERCOMING Series, "The Story of Verna Louise Williams." As a birth mother, and as an overcomer of obstacles, Vashti hopes this series speaks to those in doubts and helps them to find a way forward. She lives in Mesa, AZ with her husband, Noah, also her co-author, emotional support, true love, dishwasher, and soul mate. Perhaps not in that order.